STARSEED
to JESUS

CHASING 5D, FINDING SALVATION

SARAH-JAYNE LEE

Contents

Dedication

This book is dedicated to my Lord & Savior Jesus Christ.

Special Thanks

Family

I would like to deeply thank all my family, Lynda, Steve, John, David, Agata, Jim and Megan. Thank you to you all, for never giving up on me and always being there, no matter what. I love you all very much.

Brothers & Sisters in Christ

I have been blessed on my "New Age to Jesus" journey to be connected with so many beautiful brothers and sisters through Christ. There are too many to thank, however, I must give special thanks to the people I'm about to mention. My brother Derrik

Behler, thank you for ministering to me at the beginning of my walk, encouraging me to work out my own salvation through God's word. This helped me immensely. I'd like to thank my sister Emily Downes, for encouraging me towards reading the bible and being the first person to share part of the gospel with me. Thank you to my sister Emma Gowlett, who helped me through one of the most difficult stages of my life. Thank you to my sister Jamie Brooks, for being that special kind of friend that points you to God's word, even when it's uncomfortable. I've been blessed by your counsel and fellowship whilst writing this book. I'd also like to thank my book coach, Nicole Watt, who not only was a great support in writing this book, but now a good friend, as well as a sister in Christ.

Lastly but certainly not least, I would like to thank my church. Thank you for being supportive and for accepting me, as Christ did. Special thanks to Mark & Sue for their support.

I'm grateful to you all, my journey wouldn't have been the same without any of you. Praise God.

Foreword

I write these words with tears streaming down my cheeks because I know this book is going to be one of the hardest things for me to write and publish. I can only rely on the strength of God to get me through. It's so painful for me to think there will be so many crushed realities and dreams, hurt feelings, and disappointments for those who fully receive these words. I remember those feelings well and it certainly wasn't easy, but what I found on the other side of that discomfort was worth all of it. My prayer for you is to ultimately come to know the truth and receive it. I desire this book to be delivered with as much love and compassion as possible, whilst remaining in truth.

Over two years ago I believed I was a Starseed. I believed the essence of who I was originated from another star system and I was here to help humanity ascend to 5D earth. I would do this through healing and shifting, while working on myself in order to raise the vibration of the planet. I lived for the ascension. I was an energy worker, a priestess; a multi-dimensional healer. My mission was to remember who I was and to awaken other Starseeds on earth to do the same; I did this through my online programs and sessions. I was solid in these beliefs, as I had vivid experiences to validate them all. In my encounters with my light family, I was ascending and seeing the results whilst receiving 'divine intelligence' that appeared to be leading me on the right path.

I had come to have a deep connection to 'spirit' and was beginning to manifest the life I had always dreamt of – everything seemed to be going right. I was doing everything I could to live out my mission here on Earth. At the same time, I was here to unlearn the things that didn't serve me, to unlock my true power, and move to the next stage of enlightenment, that next vibration, and the changes in my life made me sure I was on the right path.

The truth has been one of the hardest things for me to accept in my life. Sometimes it's so much easier to live in a place where there's the most comfort, as we hold on to beliefs we desperately desire to be true, even though reality proves otherwise. Little did I realise it but as a Starseed I was living in a fantasy world. I had built such a false sense of self that it took me some time to even acknowledge that such a thing as absolute truth exists.

I've always been endlessly searching, knowing there was something more than what I knew. Finally, I can say my search for truth and meaning is now complete, but what shocked me is how, when, and where I found both. I resisted this path for many reasons, but now there's nothing more I desire than to share what I found with others, and that is salvation in Jesus Christ.

There is not only truth in Jesus, but Jesus *is* the truth, just like He told us through His own words, "I am the way, the truth, and the life; no one comes to the Father except through me".

If my old self was reading this book whilst I was practising new age, I would have likely thrown it down at this point and rolled my eyes. I once believed Christians were caught up in an old paradigm, trapped in religion and operating at a lower level of consciousness than me. How could something so old and basic as the Bible be the chalice of truth when I was practising astral travel, soul retrieval and downloading light codes? How could something so cutting-edge, innovative, and on the brink of a new dimension be false and something that's been around for so long be true? I unexpectedly discovered I had been spending all the programming and conditioning of recent years under the leading of a false light.

There was a man that once walked the earth that changed everything ... around two thousand years ago. Jesus of Nazareth stood on top of a mountain in Israel and preached the greatest sermon ever, The Sermon on the Mount. This sermon is the template that He left behind for the lost to find the truth and light, receive that light, and stay on the path of that light. Some of His words in that sermon I share here: "Enter by the narrow gate. For wide is the gate and broad is the road that leads to destruction and many that enter through it. But small is the gate and narrow the road that leads to life, and only few find it." Jesus warned us about the narrow path of true light and all the distractions will be the false light trying to take us off that path.

My hope is that this book for you at this moment in time is an entry point to the narrow path. By holding this book in your hands, you are standing right at the entrance of the gate, and I pray for your soul to enter. There is a God who has spoken: He has told us exactly who He is and how to come into relationship with Him, and He sent His only Son, Jesus, to do this for you.

I want you to know writing this book isn't fun for me. I take no enjoyment in sharing this information and potentially hurting people's feelings. But I do it because I know where this may lead: to the truth into the heart of Christ, He who loves you unconditionally. What I've come to know, even though the journey toward truth can be extremely uncomfortable, confrontational, and hard to accept, when we truly arrive there is nothing more liberating, wholesome, perfect, loving, and genuine. We are born again and receive new life. I want nothing more than for you to receive this authentic love. It was a hard reality for me to come to terms with this truth, but the rewards have been beyond anything I could ever have received. For the first time in my life, I feel light in my heart.

I never really understood the false light fully until now. I always heard about the false light, but I never knew I was part of it. How we are introduced to the teachings in New Age is different for everyone. There will be much of my journey you don't connect with. For you, it didn't happen quite like that, but I trust that there will be much of my story that is very similar to your own journey if you feel you are a Starseed. It's not my place to tell you you're not;

but I can tell you what I believe to be true through my story which made me realise the Starseed narrative is a deception.

There may be things I say in this book that challenge your reality, cause upset and even tempt you to stop reading. I encourage you to continue as there is nothing unhealthy about being challenged every once in a while. If things get tough, trust me, I am right there praying for you and assuring you there is a God who loves you deeply; that will give you strength and comfort.

A God who has been so patient with you, who loves you more than you can ever imagine and now wants your heart. I don't want to force anything on you in what I say. But the fact you are reading this book may be a sign that it's time for you to hear the voice of your heavenly Father, a voice you've likely been running away from this entire time.

Before we move on, I'd like to make it clear that among the mentors in my New Age journey, there isn't one of them I do not consider a kind person. They were caring, loving and pure intentioned. I believe they are deceived but this doesn't mean their intentions were not pure. This is my story in truth. However, I have changed the names and details of individuals to protect their identity. I do believe the majority of people today who follow the path of a lightworker genuinely feel they are doing well and have a love for people. This book isn't about slamming others or their intentions: it's about uncovering lies and revealing truth. If you're heavy into New Age, I suspect initially you will experience perhaps a range of emotions as you read on, as did I; but I continue sharing because I know where this leads: to the truth, the real light, and the endless love in Christ.

Take your time, God is patient and with you every step of the way... His way, the way of Jesus Christ. This isn't just a book: it's a journey, one I believe God has invited you to take with me.

Love Always,

Sarah-Jayne

England 2023

"And the Lord said, 'Stand at the crossroads and look; ask for the ancient paths, ask where the good way is, and walk in it, and you will find rest for your souls.'"

Jeremiah 6:16

A Cry for Affirmation

I would consider my childhood a normal one in the conventional sense, although societal norms have changed very much since those days. But you get my drift – middle-class home in an ex-council estate, fought with my two brothers, went to school like any other kid, had friends and hobbies.

As a child, I had two great loves: art and running. I loved both to death. I drove my mum crazy as a kid; any spare pad or paper I'd be there with my little designs, writing my name or practising my signature. She'd be on the telephone needing to write down a telephone number and frantically searching for a notepad with space to write because of my array of pen sketches all over them.

I was a shy little girl – one of my school reports actually described me as "painfully shy". I just loved to create; everywhere I went, I always saw opportunities to express myself through art. I remember even being on the beach once and I called my mum over so she could see my sculpture of a lady made out of sand and used cigarette butts I had gathered on the beach. Needless to say, Mum wasn't impressed but also couldn't help but laugh. But that was me, always looking at things from a creative angle and trying to make something of them.

And then there was running. Running was just the best. I felt so free and fast, and I was naturally gifted in this area. I ran everywhere and never settled with just walking. Even when my brother and I would walk alongside my mum to the shops, it was always "first one to the lamppost and back". I remember playing as kids in the street and feeling the pure joy when all the boys would have enough of football and opt to play 'run outs' – for all my USA readers – that's a slightly adapted version of Tag.

By the time I was ten, I was at a running club; at eleven, I was competing in the Under Thirteen (U13) girls running league. I soon won the Essex Championships 1500m. That's the one day I remember my dad coming to watch me; he missed the heats but saw the final – around 12 girls on the start line. As soon as the gun went I took off fast and led it from start to finish. I was just always running, thinking about running or day dreaming about becoming an Olympic athlete. The Olympics was always a really fun time in our house, as my entire family would get involved and want to watch it. During track we would all pick a lane of who we thought would win; we were a competitive family and still are in many ways. Put it this way, our monopoly board was held together by plastic tape.

As I grew up, I began to take running much more seriously. My family was pretty serious about sport too, so this fitted well as both my brothers played football at a high level as teenagers. It became a common routine for Dad to take them football and Mum to take me running. On top of this, my father worked nights and so had to sleep during some of the day time and my mum worked a full time job. Because of all this, we didn't spend that much time together as a family. Both my mother and father allocated a lot of their time to their children's sports, and for that I'm very grateful.

I remember my first ever big win. It was the school district sports with the 800m competing with girls from year 5 and 6. I was running against a girl named Laura, who was one of the fastest in Essex and a year above me. I ran a great race and I won. I remember the euphoria – it was just amazing and I just knew that's what I wanted to do for the rest of my life. From the age of eleven onwards, running wasn't just a hobby but something I needed to excel in. I learnt from a young age it was a way to get recognition, and as children we interpreted that as love. Now my parents loved me greatly, but that was my perception at the time. I gathered a collection of medals, mainly gold. Winning became the only goal and I became good at it.

But with being first comes the pressure of always needing to be the best. Most track races I used to win outright. However, as we grew older, other girls started catching up and I started to lose races. This had an impact on my confidence. I remember being so nervous before races that someone might beat me, I used to feel physically sick. I felt such pressure to win, and soon adopted the thinking that losing meant I was not good enough. Things started to deteriorate – and fast. Gradually, that shiny, sporty happy girl slowly vanished from the scene. Other kids and the culture began having a greater impact on me, and my attention moved to other things. As my interest in boys and being popular increased, I took a real bad turn.

Enter the Party Girl

A week before my fifteenth birthday, I tried my first recreational drug. At this point I had completely given up on running for my local club. Our Friday had become asking our parents for £10 for a movie and pizza, and spending that on a pack of Bacardi Breezers, hooch, or some of the harder spirits like vodka.

There was usually a big group of us, but this particular night it was just my friend Sabrina and me. We were standing outside of a pub named The Crown. Whilst we were discussing our plans for the evening, bursting out the pub's double doors came my friend Lucy's older sister, Tara. I had never spoken to Tara directly until this night, but I had been there a few times when she came and chatted to our group. I remember her confidence; she liked a drink, and she was really loud and fun. When she showed up, it was normally all eyes on her; she just seemed to be so much fun and made people laugh. It always seemed like she just knew everyone, she had such personality and people liked her. People thought of her as someone so free, without a care in the world.

I don't remember how at fifteen I even managed to get into the pub, although it became a common thing from then on. But what I do remember is my friend Sabrina passing me this rolled-up note in the toilet cubicle, and me bending down to snort a line of white powder off the back of the toilet seat. Little did I know that moment would change the course of my life dramatically. The shy, sporty, smiling, gentle and ambitious girl I was, had already been eclipsing. This I felt was the last nail in the coffin. Every focus in life changed to partying, drinking, recreational drugs, boys, raves, and music. The drugs gave me confidence. I felt like I was someone else when I took them, and people noticed me. I was sick of being the good girl that couldn't live up to everyone's expectations. After such intense training schedules and commitment to sport, it felt so good to just do things that were fun. I rebelled and massively. I even got the nick name 'Sandy' from the film Grease, as almost overnight I went from boring good girl to fun bad girl.

I learnt quickly that drinking made me popular, liked, and accepted. I wasn't only accepted but I was admired for my partying – well, by some – but in my circles, I became known as **that** girl, the fun one, the one with not a care in the world, the one that could out drink most men, and the one that you could always have a good night out with. As a lot of my close friends were boys I became one of 'the lads'.

Some nights I had too much fun. This escalated into stumbling home or sitting in a room completely stressed out I was going to have a heart attack from all the chemicals pumping around my system. There were many times I took it too far, but somehow I always seemed to pull it back around and regain balance. Some nights I just took it way too far with paranoia, memory loss, and indiscretion, especially the over sharing of my life details with strangers. I'd feel ashamed, but come next Friday, that was all forgotten and the cycle would start again.

It's funny how we can get pinned down with a character, and then notice how we get some kind of reaction from people who we desire. We interpret this as love, acceptance, friendship, self-worth, in a word, meaning. Then we associate that activity as a way of receiving that love, even though it was not really love – just felt like it. Sadly, I was championed and praised for how much alcohol I could drink, how fun I was out, and how many days I could party nonstop. That became my identity.

"And even if our gospel is veiled, it is veiled to those who are perishing."

2 Corinthians 4:3

Rock Bottom

W hen I was twenty-one, I moved to Marbella, Spain, where I got to party every day. I stayed there for five months, then came back the next year and stayed for eighteen months. Here is when it all got really out of hand: my life was one big party. I got myself into some sticky situations out there and, thank God, made it out alive. For those of you who don't know Marbella, it's renowned for its partying and glamorous lifestyle. But it can be rather pretentious. It draws a lot of people who really want to be somebody, probably for all the wrong reasons. I lived and stayed in Puerto Banús which got dubbed Port of Abuse as so many self-sabotage and feed their addictions.

I got a job serving cocktails in a bar, and again became well known for partying. Marbella was well known for both its expats and crooks. At the time I was really attracted to the gangster lifestyle, likely because I felt they commanded respect. There was a certain attraction in being the wife of a gangster, like no one could mess with you. They did what they wanted, and that kind of power appealed to me at twenty-one. I watched too many Al Pacino movies,

I think. There were some dark nights out there, ones I don't care to ever speak about. Things from Satan always seem great on the surface; they come in the most appealing packages – fun summer nights, the beach, the amazing weather, and such opulence. But under the hood, it was infested with so much darkness.

One night I got talking to one of the regular customers in the bar about wealth and growth. He drove a Lamborghini and said he would tell me how he got it. At the time I thought he was passing me the key to the rich glamorous lifestyle. A few days later he emailed me this document. It was detailing how what we think about becomes our reality and it showed exercises on visualization. I didn't know this term at the time, but he was teaching me what they refer to as the 'Law of Attraction'. He said he had the picture of that car on his wall; then he visualised the same car but in a different colour. I came to believe that what we think about and focus our energy on eventually shows up in our physical world.

This did spark my interest in personal development – and just bettering myself. I decided I was done with the Port as I couldn't keep up this lifestyle forever and it was getting the better of me. I moved back home to the UK and landed a job in a London casino. It was the perfect setting to put my law of attraction skills to work, and it seemed to really help. I then came across a book called *The Secret* and felt I had just discovered the key to the entire universe. It was similar to what I had heard before, just with much more detail. I felt this would really help me create more tip money. Looking back, it certainly encouraged me to be really nice and generous to people; this created strong bonds and so people tipped me well. Even though I was in fulltime work, on the weekend my partying lifestyle was still out of control.

Fast forward a few years, here was I sitting on my bed in my flat in Bethnal Green, East London, staring at my wardrobe. I had woken up from another heavy night of partying. I was so tired of waking up and feeling ashamed about the night before. This particular night I had no idea how I got home, but I was getting flashbacks of the things I had said to people, which made me squirm and cringe with embarrassment. I didn't want to live anymore. I hated myself.

The Onset of Depression

From the age of fifteen, cocaine and alcohol had a hold of my life and it reached the point where I couldn't break the cycle because I had never known anything different. Throughout those years there were times when I calmed down a lot. This was usually in relationships or when I focused on fitness, so it wasn't continuous. I never did it in a work environment or the like, but it was a recurring theme throughout my years and never fully went away. For the past year I had been battling depression, which really is no surprise, given all the rubbish I was putting into my system.

So, there I was just staring at my wardrobe, and in my mind, trying to contemplate what would be the best way to end my life – the most painless way. I really don't know if I was there in this space for ten minutes or two hours but I just remember those destructive thoughts. I don't think I was ever close to going through with it, but my mood was quite intense.

Then I started just asking myself how my life could ever come to this. *How did I get here?* Living was so painful but yet I felt numb. I began thinking to myself: *I don't want anyone to ever feel like this again. I wouldn't wish this on my worst enemy.* That thought persisted: ***I don't ever want anyone to feel this way.***

I genuinely felt so much compassion and understanding for anyone who had suffered depression. Drink, pornography, debt, drugs, gambling, all those things can really take a hold over our lives. Just then I remembered this burning desire to help people who felt as I did. *But wait, if I go, then how will I help these people? What will that say to them? To give up!* My brother's words from our conversation days before also kept echoing in my mind; "Sarah, the only person who can change your life is you". I will always be grateful for those words. They could have in fact saved my life: this girl had a lot more fight in her yet, so it seemed!

So there and then I made the decision that I would do everything in my power to get over this depression. I would make myself feel good again and then I would help others too! Sounds farfetched but those were my motives. Something in me just knew I was going to do this, maybe because I had the resolve not to quit. Our determination can take us a long way. I threw myself into researching just about everything I could find to help with depression and quit alcohol. I tried AA meetings for a month or so, but it never quite felt my path. The popular internet search results for overcoming depression were "meditation, yoga, mindfulness, healthy eating", "low consumption of alcohol" and "exercise" (obviously), so this was the start of 'Operation Feel Good'.

I did a post speaking openly about my depression on my Facebook; it was almost like 'coming out'. Some people were shocked. They thought I had it all together and loving life. I got a ton of support. I do believe God put it upon my heart to genuinely want to help people. I remember just not wanting anyone else to have to go through this so much; it was soul-destroying. Like many others in New Age, my intentions were always pure from the beginning. However, I've now come to realise that no amount of good intentions were able to prevent me from being drawn into darkness.

My Facebook post got featured in the readers' letter section of *Grazia*, a popular women's magazine in the UK. Other friends on my Facebook page started to reach out and say they had been going through the same. Obviously, I wasn't pleased for them, but this did give me some comfort and really made me realise how common this mental condition is – except no one is talking about it. A fresh purpose and hope entered my life, and I ran with it as best as I could.

One of those people to reach out was my childhood friend, Sabrina, who used to join me at the pub. We'd lost touch for many years, so this was our first interaction in quite a while. She had also been going through some hard times herself. She told me about this woman she went to see who was amazing and now she felt so much better, I asked for more details, but Sabrina said she couldn't really explain it and said to just go and that I wouldn't regret it. It didn't take much persuading; at this point if it had even a slight chance of helping with my depression, I was in. I was desperate and felt I had nothing to lose.

Energy Healing

On the day of the appointment, I was hopeful. I remember this woman who answered the door with such a warm and lovely smile. I was a bit nervous and felt slightly awkward as I didn't even know what to expect. Valerie was her name; she was an 'energy healer' and the session was focused on emotion. You can imagine how profound this session was for me. For over ten years, the only way I knew how to deal with any emotion was alcohol. Had a good day at work? Let's go celebrate down at the pub. Bad day? I'm going to need a drink. For over ten years I had never actually dealt with any emotion whatsoever; it had all been pushed down with poison. This is so common. Some people may use food, others cigarettes, alcohol, shopping and so on. From a young age, emotions have a dramatic effect on our mood and behaviour, it's no wonder that even as adults many of us do not manage our emotions in a healthy way.

Valerie was different from anyone that I'd known before. She wore this long silky flowing kaftan with her thick long grey hair draping down her shoulders. She seemed well kept and her smile was so friendly. Her home smelt of potions and oil; it was adorned with crystals, incense, figurines and pictures of angels and candles. It seemed like another world and it sparked so much curiosity within me.

In this session we did a timeline style therapy centred on the 'inner child'. Here you work with memories in the subconscious that have had a deep impact on the beliefs you hold about yourself, about others, and the world. I had a memory come up from my childhood of my running and not feeling good enough. I felt an instant release. It felt good to cry and finally acknowledge feelings I'd been carrying for a long time.

After this session, things felt very different. I remember looking at the sky, the trees, and everything just felt so joyful. I realised that there was some healing needed for me about things that had happened throughout my life, things I hadn't wanted to face and, quite frankly, had run away from. I later came to learn that apparently this was a spiritual awakening, and the depression I felt was what is known as the 'dark night of the soul'. It is believed this is a period of darkness we go through before a rebirth. It's like the old self is leaving in order for the new self to emerge. Think of the caterpillar that must go into the cocoon before it comes into all its splendour. This gave meaning to my depression.

Following my appointment, I was given links to motivational speaker, Louise Hay, and other helpful resources. I would often fall asleep to Louise Hay and her meditations. This got me exploring online and I was soon discovering an entirely new world. It was thrilling really; there was so much out there to explore. I became engrossed in the pursuit of inner peace, stepping into my power, self-love, and healing. A month or so later I booked in with Valerie again for another session.

We did more on the inner child, releasing what no longer served me. It was in this session I was told I was a Starseed.

"For the time is coming when people will not endure sound teaching, but having itching ears they will accumulate for themselves teachers to suit their own passions."

2 Timothy 4:3

You're Special

O ne may think that the moment I heard I was a Starseed for the first time, it would instantly resonate with me. This was far from the truth. I thought it was a bit far-fetched and if I'm honest, a tad crazy. But I came to trust Valerie. Besides being kind, she had already shown me things I didn't believe at first, which later appeared to be true. For those of you who are unaware, people who think they are Starseeds believe their souls originated in another planet, and in another life their soul chose to volunteer to come to earth to teach love and be the light.

How I really gravitated toward this were the words, "You're special", something I'd been longing to hear all my life. Looking back and unaware of my deep need at the time, I clung to those words for the rest of my New Age journey. Deep down I had always desired recognition, to be special, and feel like my life had meaning. So even though I didn't really believe the Starseed identity instantly, it didn't take long for me to be convinced I truly was one. It was all those unusual experiences, conversations, and ultimately the need to satisfy my deep longing to be special in some way that did it.

When I found New Age, I was in a state of deep regret over my life. Here was I approaching thirty and realising that my life had been all about chasing instant pleasure, searching for things in all the wrong places like bars and clubs, and nothing to show for my years. I was depressed and seeking answers and meaning. The healing work gave me relief and allowed me to *capture* my emotions. I sought healing therapies and teachers that could help.

I got into following different New Age Spiritual teachers, and my focus and knowledge changed over the years depending on what I was working through at that time. Learning the healing modalities for myself and then the Starseed narrative was just the piece missing for me to put a frame round the perfect picture. Now it all came together and made sense. It allowed me to not only accept the past but to validate and justify it. There were plausible answers and reasons for it all. My partying, bad choices, poor judgement and lack of responsibility were all validated, and I didn't have to take responsibility for any of it. This was self-compassion which is important to a degree, but it was also complete denial and acceptance of the consequences of my choices and actions. Not only that, but I was told this was also all totally meant to be! These were all such comforting answers at the time because they affirmed me.

I was told from various different channels that apparently many Starseeds suffer from alcohol, drugs, substance abuse, and other toxic patterns. The reasoning behind this is that they were originally from planets where there is a much higher consciousness of love, and they are not used to such low density energy on earth. Therefore, to cope with this low vibration, Starseeds will likely turn to addictions or other forms of sabotage. This narrative made me comfortable with my past and accept it was something meant to be – well, let's face it – I fitted the mould perfectly. Looking at it now, I can see the holes in this belief system: I became the problem, but then the solution. I was very vulnerable and was open to most things if they would make me feel better. Looking back, it's clear the type of subject the Starseed narrative was targeting.

Are You a Starseed?

It's not uncommon to find many blogs or posts flying around spiritual communities with the headline "How to know you're a Starseed". They differ in style, but most would include the following:

- You've always felt like you don't really belong (the most popular).

- You're an empath.

- You're intuitive.

- You are searching for life purpose and deeper meaning.

- You're spiritual.

- People tend to call you sensitive.

- You have psychic abilities.

- You are drawn to conspiracy theories.

- You're a truth seeker.

- You have a love for nature.

- You're drawn to a vegan or vegetarian diet.

- You love animals.

- You enjoy your own company.

- You're drawn to crystals.

- You feel homesick and can't explain why.

- You feel you've lived many lives.

- You have feelings of loneliness.

- You are wise beyond your years.

- You are drawn to ancient alien programs or books.

The interesting thing is, of course, that most of the above will resonate with most people with a similar background to myself. In the New Age I believed I was an Empath; this meant that my energy field was hypersensitive and I would naturally take other people's problems, feelings, or emotions on as if they were my own. I know this now to be a learned behaviour we acquire from young as a result of certain family dynamics and other relationships. As children we take on what's going on around us naturally. This is part of growing up, not this energy vibration thing where our energy is deemed to be more sensitive than others.

With hindsight, this list doesn't really signify anything out of the norm at all. Who doesn't love nature and animals? A very slim percentage of the population. Every single one of the signs on the list would look very attractive and relatable to someone that is moving out of depression and looking for deeper meaning to life. It strikes a chord with someone with a deep wanting. I remember I would ponder on some of them and, even though I had never even thought of the topic before, I was finding myself relating to it. For example, I felt like I'd lived many lives; my thought process was ... *Well, I guess I've never really thought about it, but I have been told I'm wise beyond my years. So I guess so.* These things just don't seem to be that dissimilar to anyone who is simply interested in spirituality; it seems now such a far cry to interpret these points as signs that we are hybrid aliens here on earth to save humanity.

Over the next few years, I threw myself into this new spiritual life I had discovered. It seemed the more I learned, the more I healed and developed both in my character and spirit. It felt like the best buffet you could ever go to. Anything and everything was available to you with such unique lessons and inner power to unlock. It was exciting coming across new healing modalities or 'secret knowledge' because each one offered some type of power or esoteric wisdom yet to be revealed. It was a continuous treasure hunt where there's never-ending treasure to find.

I ventured into learning different spiritual practices such as those taught at the Vipassana Retreat in Bali. This is a silent retreat where you practice a meditation technique named Vipassana, apparently taught by Buddha. Although I remember experiencing a lot of fear on this retreat, the organisers told me it was all part of the healing, and so I stuck it out. It was on this retreat that I again processed more memories, more trauma from my past, acknowledged them, and 'let go'. I also received 'divine guidance'. I believe this is where I really opened myself up to other spirits, who told me clearly I had to go back home and learn a certain healing modality and help others heal the way I had been healed. I followed that guidance and enrolled on the training course right away. It was time for me to step into my 'light-worker' role.

Valerie had also advised me to go learn reiki as it would change my relationship with energy. I progressed through Reiki One and Two and within three years became a Master. My Reiki Two attunement was where I met my friend Mark who quickly became one of my friends and main mentors. Through Mark, the Starseed topic came up again. He had psychic abilities and confirmed I was one. Because of all the things that had happened up to this point, all the healing and spiritual experiences I had encountered – I was more open to this Starseed topic now. It still felt a bit weird; but I had been on this path for a while now and most things seemed strange at first – like not talking for ten days at the Vipassna retreat, spiritual awakening, and many more discoveries.

Ectlana and Me

Over the course of the next year, more and more knowledge kept unfolding about this Starseed belief. But it wasn't until I had very real, authentic experiences during some energy sessions that I then fully converted to this belief system.

Mark and I got on really well. We both loved being spiritual and doing energy work; we both didn't have children and had the time to explore the spiritual realm. He has been doing this type of work for twenty years. He was like a fountain of knowledge, and I was in awe of all the things he knew. If I came across something new, I'd mention it to him, and he would more than likely have a deep understanding of it already. He taught me how to set up energy sessions (where we intend to work in the spiritual realm) using different methods of protection. He showed me how I was in control of my energy field and how to step more into my power. He was so in touch with my spirit that he always understood where I was in my journey.

We would meet regularly to do healing sessions. I remember there were a few very intense months where I felt my mental and emotional health were becoming so challenged. I was going through some really intense healing, and incidents in my past were coming up in order for me to address. So much pain, trauma as well as limiting beliefs needed to be cleared. I remember during this time I was triggered so frequently; it felt like I was constantly going through deep emotional healing, working through a lot of my 'blocks'. There is an element of truth in this as clearing trauma and healing will have a positive effect. But now, knowing Jesus, I look back and can see how unnecessary and dangerous this exploration really was.

I'm certain Satan has researched the body, mind, and spirit to such a degree he has managed to produce modalities and methods that appear to give the same effect as a deep relationship with the Father. The concept of 'inner child' seems to be traced back to Carl Jung, who was an occultist. In his psychoanalysis, he discovered that our pysche is split into various archetypes, the inner child being one. Now, out of all of the modalities I practised, this is the first one I was ever trained in; to me by far this is the most effective in terms of working through trauma. However, my main concern is that a lot of these discoveries are from imagination and are really out-of-body experiences. I now do not think it's healthy to view ourselves in terms of split identities and personas. Also, once we seem to open the door to the inner child, it seems to never settle as more and more issues keep coming to light. I don't think this is healthy on a long-term basis and do touch on the topic again in a later chapter.

One day during an energy session guided by Mark, something that very profound happened. I had just experienced one of the deepest and hardest releases of emotion I'd ever had and had been crying intensely for at least an hour. Profound experiences always happened right after a deep session; it's almost like a spiritual reward after a deep release, kind of like, *Now that you've just cleared so much low-level energy, welcome to your new level of vibration!* My emotions were highly charged then, and I was more open. There was some music playing to help draw out my emotions, too.

On this particular occasion, a light being came in. During our sessions I would always tell Mark what was going on and he would ask me questions and guide me through it. I told him what I could see, and he said, "Why have they come to you?" I instantly cried. I remember the emotion. It felt like home ... but more on feelings later.

With this light being, it was like I was communicating with her just through energy, not words. It was me in another dimension. As this point, space and time didn't exist for me, and I thought that my Starseed self in another dimension and time reality was trying to make contact. She told me her name, Ectlana; this was transmitted in 'light language' – that's the nearest I could transliterate the sound. This experience took me from 'I'm not sure' to 'I'm all in' for the Starseed journey. *How could I not believe this now that I have experienced this being!!* The Starseed topics opened up a new and exciting arena and it seemed as thrilling as a fantasy. I researched more online and found so many people who believed they were Starseeds, and I found many of them relatable. *So this isn't just a crazy idea; this is real and there are so many living it to prove it*, so I thought at the time.

After meeting Ectlana, I felt the buzz for more spiritual experiences. I was hooked. There were so many activations, downloads, and upgrades; it was like a constant quest to excel and ascend, things like activating your twelve-strand DNA, downloading new keys and codes, light language, and working with earth grids, to name a few. I basically fell into this delusion that I was really a hybrid alien, a high-performing super human that had all this power, but it was currently lying dormant, and this ascension path was all about waking up and activating it!

I researched Starseeds in earnest, the reason we are here and our supposed mission on earth. I started to believe that I had chosen to come here through my own choice I made in another dimension (another star system); the earth was in trouble, and she had put out the call to other star systems for volunteers to go help on this planet. I started to believe in a great awakening of humanity and how my existence on earth at this time was part of the larger plan. Beings from star systems such as the Pleiades, Mintaka, Arcturus and others had all received the offer. If they chose to accept the invitation to go to earth, they would experience new conditions such as these low-level emotions like grief, guilt, and shame.

Their mission is to be born into this world, not knowing anything about their origin, with amnesia blocking everything they truly are. However, at some stage in their earth life journey, they would experience an 'awakening' and come to remember who they are. They would then spend the rest of their human life raising their vibration and teaching humans about love. They would do this through healing, and clearing all those low-level energies through different healing modalities, plant medicines, and spiritual practices.

There are so many facets to the Starseed narrative. One account refers to 'The Fall', a new age version of the Adam and Eve's fall in the Bible. This mainly concerns Atlantis which was supposedly a civilisation that was operating in 5D, which is a high vibration of love. Apparently after the fall of Atlantis, the earth went into a low level of vibration known as 3D – this is a dense vibration. There is another density, 4D, which, apparently, we need to travel through in order to reach the desired destination, 5D. 4D is where all the healing happens, the lower vibrations are released, and we are working on ourselves. Starseeds believe that by doing all the inner work and clearing trauma, they are raising their vibration and later that of the planet, so humanity can reach this 5D state of bliss, which is the ultimate goal. This state can vary in names, but some call it, 'The New Golden Age' or 'The Age of Aquarius' or '5D earth'. So, effectively, Starseeds believe they are healing their own traumas to raise the vibration of the planet and usher in the new age. There are many different theories, but all refer to entering an age of utopia, where people are whole and completely healed, where everyone is in alignment with the vibration of love, and there is peace and harmony in society. This is often connected to Lemuria, too, another lost land believed to have been in 5D until it plummeted and fell.

This is typically what is meant by 'New Age', that is, beings working towards this high vibrational existence on Earth. I never would have considered myself as 'New Age' when I was practising. I simply thought I was sovereign and had my own beliefs and path. But what I didn't see at the time was that everything I believed was actually from channelled materials, teachers, books, and my own channelling of 'spirits'. I will expand on this in later chapters.

At this point in my journey, I didn't believe in Satan either – and I actually found people who did quite comical. I felt they were just in 3D, and I used to feel sorry for these 'trapped' people. But writing this now, I know the truth and the truth is, the 5D agenda is all part of Satan's lies. He is real and this is all to usher in the one world religion, known in the Bible as the end times. I truly believed that Christians were caught up in an old paradigm, trapped in religion, and operating at a lower level of consciousness than us. I didn't outwardly think this or speak of it, but the belief that I was a Starseed made me feel superior to other people: somehow they didn't get it as they were not at my level of enlightenment. I even looked down on family members and friends that I felt were living in a 3D world.

As far as I was concerned, I was a powerful being, here to unlock that power and help others to do the same. And it appeared I was on the right path. I was beginning to manifest the life I had been working towards (or so it appeared). But things are not always the way they **appear**.

"You live in the midst of deception; in their deceit they refuse to acknowledge me," declares the LORD."

Jeremiah 9:6

My New Name

I really felt I was living a dream. People were finding value from my services and my business started to gain traction. I never needed to be some internet sensation but I did always desire to live the life I cherished. My work of helping to raise the vibration of the planet had become a full-time way to also make a living, and to do that I did need some sort of following. In the new age I referred to any kind of divine guidance as 'spirit' and, since 'spirit' had always told me I was here to awaken the Starseeds, I always knew I would only appeal to Starseeds, which were the minority. I called myself a 'multi-dimensional healer'.

What this looked like for me was a 10-15-hour week. I know that sounds crazy but that's all I worked. I'd have a program running which was a 60-90 min session a week with two to three long-term clients and some one-off sessions. I was never one to charge high ticket prices, but I made enough to keep me going; I also sold crystals which brought in additional income. My work was so easy; I never really had to put much work into content as everything was channelled. However, I didn't see it as working only 15 hours a week, as most of my time was dedicated to healing and clearing "what no longer served me", so I viewed this as a big part of my business. My viewpoint was, *I am my business and so the more I grow, the more my business supports me.*

Because I was here for the ascension, 'the universe' was in a way paying me to heal and work on myself. After all, it was my service to humanity, so my business was about me: I was the focal point. I was to work on myself and focus on my own ascension, and then, naturally, I could guide others to do the same. I cringe now looking back at the self-centredness of it all – even all my advertising which was a constant flow of selfies on my feed.

But at the time I didn't see it. I truly felt my time had finally come: all those healing sessions, all those tears I released. I was here for the Starseeds; it was my job to lead people into discovering their power, to discover their Starseed and then helping them share their gifts with others. I was here not only for my own ascension but to assist people with their own personal ascension to usher in this new golden age. On the surface, I was living out my destiny.

Over the space of a year I had a few encounters with the light being Ectlana. Once I had built trust there, I started working a lot more with her. On one particular occasion, I was in an energy session and had just bought a fluorite point crystal; this is where I received my new name, 'Ectlana Mage'. As soon as I heard it, my eyes opened and I took a deep breath in. It instantly resonated with my soul and I just knew it had been my name all along. Soon after, I changed all my social media and business names to Ectlana Mage; and that was when my business gained more attention. This was such an exciting step in my work; but now looking back this was a clear sign that this seducing spirit was deepening its influence on my words, actions and being.

My activity didn't feel like work because it was fun and enjoyable but I was serious about it. In my mind the ascension was real, and the future of humanity depended on people waking up. As 'spirit' used to tell me, I was here for the Starseeds, and it was my mission to help them awaken and unlock their inner power. This obviously involved telling people they were Starseeds for the first time. (How this makes me cringe now!) This took some doing to get over, not from the embarrassment of sounding completely bonkers to people, but also because this resonated with some people and they actually went down this path. It was hard for me to accept that you can have the best intentions and truly love people, and then find out you misdirected them down a false trail.

I recently saw an old post from one of my programs that made me cry, not because of the work I'd done but because of the community we had developed. In one course, in particular, we were moving into inner child work, and we all bought care bear teddies like we had as kids. There were some fun memories with lovely people, and I miss those kinds of moments dearly. You see, not everything I taught was deceptive. There were still valuable exercises to process emotion through journalling and self-awareness exercises, things I would still do today. But much of it, to my regret, was leading people astray, especially those with whom I held deep friendships and shared very fond memories. It took me a long time to realise I'm forgiven – but I did get there in the end; thank You Jesus. If you are one of those people and I haven't told you this already, I am extremely sorry and all I can say is I didn't realise I was deceived by the spirits I was working with. I hope you can find it in your heart to forgive me.

Signs of Ascending

I think it's important I also mention the ascension 'symptoms'. Now these really vary depending on the source, but the main focus always seems to be on recognising changes in our mood, physical body, health, and emotional and mental wellbeing. This usually happened after a healing session, or some kind of energetic portal or a full moon. Every full moon and new moon I used to do a ceremony in my group. The new moon was always about manifesting, while the full moon was about clearing and releasing. The full moons were sometimes hard to handle because there were always many of us with intense emotions or mental states. It wasn't unusual for people to feel they were having a crisis. They were unsettled and restless. and emotional lows were common. This was when we all used to reach for a meditation, activation, upgrade, or pay for an energy healing session.

After my full moon sessions, people used to say they felt so much better. I did too when I did these things. It was always that next release, to clear the next 'block': you just had to work through your triggers and what was coming up. What a way to live!! I was totally unaware it was voluntary emotional distress at the time, but I was led to believe I had chosen this path in another dimension. These Ascension Symptoms are said to be as follows:

- Feeling highly emotional, such as sadness or anger (intense triggers)

- Loss of identity

- Difficulty in focusing

- Blocked throat

- Self-talk and inner dialect

- Hearing spirit

- Body aches, pains, headaches and fatigue

- Intense dreams – could be dark as when clearing low energy

- Trouble sleeping, insomnia

- Sleep paralysis

- Heart palpitations

- Ringing in ears

- Feeling 'out of control'

- Bouts of depression

I had experienced nearly all of the above. Now I see them as symptoms of demonic oppression. It's worrying how I could have thought all of the above were good signs.

At this stage, I had worked with and was trained by some respected teachers within the New Age community. I felt confident in my mission here on earth and was witnessing myself becoming more and more powerful. I believed I was a sovereign being, coming into my power, able to collapse timelines, perform astral travel, manipulate space and time, use my sexual energy to manifest ... and so much more. I was a Priestess like I had been many lifetimes before in Atlantis, Lemuria, and Ancient Egypt.

Little did I know, I wasn't becoming more powerful. I was just basing my happiness on outside circumstances and how people responded to what I was doing. The deeper I went, the more blinded I became.

"Love is patient, love is kind. It does not envy, it does not boast, it is not proud. It does not dishonor others, it is not self-seeking, it is not easily angered, it keeps no record of wrongs. Love does not delight in evil but rejoices with the truth. It always protects, always trusts, always hopes, always perseveres. Love never fails."

1 Corinthians 13:4-8

Twin Flames

If I were to go through my entire testimony, it would be volume 1-10 – seriously! But I felt God really leading me to write this book with a focus on the Starseed aspect. I've included the 'twin flame' topic in this, as many Starseeds will also relate to the twin flames and it's a huge part of my coming to Christ. Some reading this may well know already there is great deception in that area. I know one of the main Starseeds accounts on social media did unravel some news on this – funnily enough, it was very shortly after I went public with my twin flame deception video on YouTube.

I had a session with a good friend of mine, who was a Starseed too, and I respected her at the time for her energy work. We decided to do regular swap sessions, so we could both grow, and effectively ascend. As she was well versed in the twin flame topic, we did a session where we actually called in my twin flame. About a month later I was doing a new moon ritual, and this particular month I decided I wanted to manifest my perfect partner. I wrote that I desired a boyfriend and described all the qualities I wanted in this person. Now, I can't actually believe I thought it was appropriate for someone to live up to a list of ideals – I mean that's part of the problem just there, isn't it? We get to the point where we start to manifest people by lists; these are people not objects to fulfil our every desire. The concept of 'twin flames' is very common on the new age path. It's similar to soul mates but much more intense. The theories differ slightly but you'll find the same core information throughout the variations.

Apparently, we were all born from stars. Before we become, what is known as human life, the star splits into two. The essence of that star is our soul going through the gates to start life. Not everyone is a twin flame; some stars do not split, but, essentially, if they do, that means someone somewhere is your other half. That person is also known as your twin flame, the other half of your soul.

As the narrative goes, many Starseeds are believed to be twin flames. Due to the frequencies that need to be raised on the planet, many twin flame reunions are happening in this lifetime because together they raise the vibration of the planet many times higher. This reunion is usually intense: like meeting part of yourself, and in the twin flame theory, that's true. There's typically a passionate instant attraction, normally followed by a whirlwind fairy tale romance. This is followed by a major conflict and then possibly a separation. This is apparently due to the low vibrations and trauma both flames carry in this world. With the pair reflecting this to each other and triggering each other, it usually gets very heated, very hard to manage and, all of a sudden, things can go from amazing love in paradise to falling apart.

This then will usually lead to the twin flame separation, where each needs to go and do the inner work on themselves. Twin Flame relationships are renowned for being really intense and hard to navigate through emotionally; this is said to happen because it's meant to bring up your darkest wounding and pain. However, only those who work on themselves can get through it and not all twin flames will do that, so there's a big emphasis on 'doing the work'. Once the inner work is complete, those lower vibrations between the two get cleared and this will energetically pull them back into reunion. The tie is still strong because they share the same soul in a sense. When they work individually on becoming whole, they're really working on the partnership as twin flames becoming whole, and so back into union.

It is said that not all twin flames are meant to come into divine union. Some are meant to just heal each other into becoming whole so they can move on to their own path. Others are meant to be in divine union for the greater good of the planet. Looking back, it's heartbreaking to imagine how twin flame unions are believed to be an important part to the great awakening and ascension into the 5D earth.

Twin Flame narratives like to twist scripture. Consider Mark 10:8: "And the two will become one flesh; so they are no longer two, but one flesh." When we read the entire passage, we can see it's referring to when two believers who marry become one flesh. By contrast, the twin flame concept is so far from God's design, it's not even relatable. It is said that when twin flames make love, they release a high vibrational energy that again helps raise the vibration of the planet. This encourages intercourse with your flame outside of marriage. This I now recognise to be another way of pulling people away more from God. God is so clear about His instructions for sexual intimacy to be only within the marriage covenant. His structure for intimacy and family life is so beautiful, it's so sad the twin flame narrative encourages the opposite. The twin flame relationship is already openly known to be an unhealthy relationship that will bring up much pain and encouraging sexual intercourse with that person adds to the pain. There are just so many aspects of the Twin Flame narrative that are so damaging and have long lasting effects.

Shadow Work

I now want to talk about a process called 'shadow work', which is massively used in twin flame healing therapy. There's a lot to this with many layers. Simply put, it's the belief that what you see in others is a reflection of yourself; everything is a mirror. For example, if you feel others are running away, or scared of commitment, they are just a reflection of you. So you need to ask yourself what aspects of your life you are running away from. How are you scared to commit to yourself? What part of you is scared? If your friend is really angry with you, then they are showing you there is anger inside of you somewhere. It's like the universe shows you what you have to work on through other people, they will mirror back to you, what's inside of you.

This then moves into the belief we are all 'one' and all 'connected'. What a dangerous way to live!! Seriously do not go there: you'll be forever analysing or justifying things through a self-centred lens. Like all deception, there are elements of truth in saying we are all connected. Yes, we are all connected in the sense that we are all made in the image of God. But shadow work leads to an unhealthy state in that everything you see in others is about you, and soon enough your life and universe becomes all about you too. I thought Shadow work was truth because I could always find something, it seemed to 'work', but now I can see it from another perspective. For example, if I see two cars next to each other and both have one headlight missing, that doesn't mean the two cars are connected. It simply means they both have a similar issue or characteristic. As humans, we all have and will experience a broad range of emotions in life, from grief, to anger, to love, to joy. This doesn't mean we are connected or a reflection; it means we are alike – which we are by nature.

If you look at everyone's traits and emotion and look for that in yourself, you'll be sure to find it if you look hard enough, even if you must go years back, because you're human, too, so likely to have had an experience with the same emotion or treated in a similar way. That one was such a head bend to come out of as I had trained myself to look at everything in this connected way. With twin flames, this connection is stronger than ever as we believe the other person (our twin flame) is part of us anyway. So then, by focusing on our other half and our relationship, we are expected to acknowledge and heal those parts of ourselves that they reflect back to us, and thus we become whole. There is no real explanation to how it's supposed to go. Some say by working on yourself, you heal your flame too; others say one of the flames can stop progressing because they don't 'do the work'. This doesn't really even make sense if you both are meant to be so connected.

Can Darkness and Light Merge?

Again, wholeness is one of the key words in the New Age. People are always looking to become whole. The irony is that in order to become whole, apparently we need to accept and embrace our darkness. Shadow work promotes being comfortable with our darkness. This is in line with the yin & yang, night & day; this means there is light and darkness in everything which brings balance. This teaching does seem rather odd now though as many who believe this, also reject the God of the Old Testament. So accepting our darkness is not all love and light. There's a stage on the ascension path where you think you are evolving as you realise that to reject parts of yourself you don't like – for example, jealously, insensitivity, manipulation and so on – isn't fully accepting and loving ourselves. So our evolution is all about integrating these discordant elements so we can become whole.

But how do you integrate darkness and light? Will two parallel lines eventually merge? Jesus makes a clear distinction between darkness and light. He says, "I am the light of the world. Whoever follows me will not walk in darkness, but will have the light of life" (John 8:12).

I can now see how this is being rolled out on the larger scale. When we are comfortable with and accept the dark, and when we believe we are all one collectively, this sets us up for the acceptance of the darker religions so that they can be more socially acceptable and integrated into society. Satanism is one such religion and so occultism and witchcraft. I suspect that how this will take shape in the future on a collective scale is society will embrace the darker religions. We can lovingly accept such religions as they teach there is no light without darkness. Therefore the darkness has its rightful place: we are not to fear this but to accept this, because it just is.

Now that I am following Christ I now see clearly. Yes, I don't need to be afraid of darkness; however, I don't need to accept the darkness to know the light. Jesus is the light; He is the way and there is no balance of darkness required for me to walk in Christ. The Bible says there is no darkness in Him. Jesus did not call us to embrace our darker side: He called us to become holy, like Him. There is not one teaching of Jesus that remotely refers to any type of instruction for shadow work. Quite the opposite. Jesus warned of the dark and preached to follow the light and light only. No integration, no merging of the two: follow the light.

Admittedly, there were positive things that came from the twin flame work I did such as my ability to become self-aware. I actually started to analyze how my feelings about myself had an effect on others, so I'm not suggesting for a moment this work doesn't have a beneficial effect. But there's where the trap is. And that's the entire reason why deception exists because it's truth mixed with lies. There needs to be a degree of truth and results to make the philosophy credible.

My Twin Flame and Me

At this point in my journey I was feeling, looking and being the best I'd ever felt in years, and I was finally achieving things in life. During my morning dog walks, I was receiving messages from 'spirit'. One morning it was very clear and concise: "Put on a Reiki Level One workshop for this weekend". It was the beginning of the week. I would never normally put on something this late, especially for an in-person event; but by now, when spirit spoke to me in such a way, I had learned to follow the guidance and move, even when it didn't make sense.

On the day of the workshop, there were only two attendees, one of my friends, Caroline, who is thankfully now a sister in Christ, and another guy, Toni, who had been following me on Youtube. He had been watching my videos for a while and we had some interaction. Judging by his Facebook account I had the expectation he was already awake or having an awakening.

The Reiki workshop was in October and by December, Toni and I were officially together. Things were moving so quickly, and I was on top of the world. It had been so long since I had been in a relationship. I had dated on the very rare occasion, but I had not been in a committed relationship with anyone for seven years. This was mainly because of all the spiritual things I had been doing, and focusing on myself. Then, when I went public about my Starseed beliefs, I thought many men would be put off, so I just got comfortable on my own.

At the reiki workshop, the energy between us was so electrifying, I felt it was divinely orchestrated. My friend Caroline said she was sure something was going to happen between us. He was the answer to my new moon manifestation ritual. When I met him, it appeared he met every single point on my list. I was on Cloud 9. The stars had finally aligned. All the inner work had finally paid off! I was manifesting and attracting my dream life, and everything was perfect.

Toni was the icing on the cake. He not only accepted my Starseed side, he embraced it. He was so engaging, intriguing and different. He wore really unique and unusual clothes, had Italian-like olive skin and had shoulder length brown hair. He embraced his weirdness, which as a Starseed attracted me like moth to a flame. We had the same interests and so much in common. He was spiritual and open minded. I believed we were destined to be together and the best bit he was crazy about me and wasn't afraid to show it. We always used to text each other, and say the same thing at once and laugh about it.

He told me he loved me after three weeks. At first this did seem intense, but I was so caught up in the romance of it all and it was moving so quickly, my emotions were heightened. Days later I told him the same. At the same time, I remember feeling a red flag deep down. I was thinking to myself, *How can I love him when I don't really know him* ? But then the twin flame soul mate connection link made it all the more understandable. I just felt as if we'd been together for years. That gave me permission to run with it and get lost in it all. It was all right to do that in a way as on this spiritual path not everything needed to make sense logically. I just had to follow my heart.

We spent many nights just cuddling and being together; this was always accompanied by beautiful 'spiritual' music, with deep meaningful words. I never realised how much this was really adding to the intensity of the relationship. I used to lie there and get so swept away in it all. When you lie there in bed with someone and listen to deep music singing about love, it's hard not to think those words are being shared between the two of you.

In these moments I would have said my life felt like a fairy tale. After years of striving and inner work, I was starting to see the life I had always dreamed of take shape, and this man appeared to be everything I desired. Not only was he not intimidated by my ambition, he supported it. He was fun and believed in the Ascension. At first, I felt a sense of security with him, and we had so much in common. It was wild that we were thinking the same things at the same time. When we cuddled, I felt so much comfort. Spirit always showed me one of those candles in my head that you see of the man and the woman intertwined: the candle also represents a flame and so I believed I was receiving the message from spirit that this man was my flame.

I just couldn't believe how my life had changed. I was becoming my own poster girl for turning your life around: a girl with no hope, drinking and depressed, who then discovered her mission here on earth, unlocked her divinity and was now teaching others to do the same. What success!! My programs seemed to be really helping people as well; I was receiving frequent downloads on guidance for the business, my weight was at its best it had ever been, and here was a man who seemed to adore me and I him. Everything was finally coming together. I started to feel like the powerful woman I always knew was inside of me. I was starting to feel like finally I had found my place.

As well as creating my own programs, I was investing heavy in New Age business coaches. I was chasing (I thought attracting) more spiritual experiences, income, results and power. The more powerful I was becoming, the more powerful I sought to become. In reality, I was just moving further and further away from God – blinded by a matrix of confusion, of lies coming in from every angle, a false world, so out of touch with reality.

Often I would wake in the morning and spend some quiet time meditating, channelling or a card pull – basically connecting with spirit. This one particular morning I remember getting up out of my bed and making my way to my yoga mat, where I sat crossed legged in a relaxed position. This time I heard something unusual ... a voice said, "You've lost your way, child." The words were very clear and caught me by surprise. It didn't come to me like the usual audible voice – it felt like it came through my inner being. I wondered what that could mean. *How could I have possibly lost my way? Life has never been better. I have never been happier!!* I instantly dismissed it and took the necessary steps to clear my space. Everything seemed to be in my favour, and I felt like I couldn't put a step wrong as the universe was just supporting me in everything. To be honest, some days I felt like I needed to pinch myself to tell myself it was all happening.

Too bad I didn't as that would have prepared me better for what was to come.

"Then you will know the truth, and the truth will set you free."

John 8:32

The Crash

L ife is full of moments. Most of them just pass us by, gone forever; but some remain vivid in our mind. One of these moments was an evening at home, alone. This was the day I really found the truth about the twin flame narrative. I discovered the behaviour of covert narcissism and the dynamics of being in a relationship with a covert narcissist, and it shocked me to the core. It was the exact template for a twin-flame relationship. My new age bubble of reality was soon to burst.

That evening, I had scheduled a call with Toni. After months of complete bliss, we had hit a rocky patch and fast. We weren't together, but I was trying to make it work. I was confused by our relationship at this stage: we weren't officially together but at the same time, we were also acting in certain ways that were more than friends, speaking often on the phone and planning things together. When we split up he said he felt like he was losing his best friend. I couldn't really understand this at the time as we'd only ever known each other in a romantic way. But I guess he just was saying we got on so well.

There was much optimism on my side as we had both agreed to go together on the long weekend we had booked. We could still cancel and get our money back at this stage, but he chose to still go, so this sent me the signal of hope. At the same time, I was confused as we weren't together, and I started to wonder if he was just expecting to be intimate. We had only recently split. I knew that it was unlikely he would agree to go away with me if it was 100 percent over as the cabin we would be sharing a room.

We planned a call to speak about the trip. I was excited as I had been doing a lot of research on the energy of the land there. But mostly I couldn't wait to speak to him. I really deep down wanted him back and I couldn't quite understand how our relationship was moving and how we weren't together.

He seemed different on the call than he had been over text. He seemed excited about certain things but very distant and uninterested in general. He also kept saying, "Is that all you want?" as if trying to get me off the call. I was confused from all the mixed messages and just simply asked if he genuinely wanted to go on this trip. Of course this led to the topic of getting back together. The conversation went back and forth; he was being so unclear and vague, with just more mixed messages. I was getting so tired and run down from all the confusion and conflicting things he was saying that I pushed for further clarity. I just needed to know for my own sake, as being apart felt so painful. It ended with him saying very sternly "I know you're not the one for me".

My world stopped. A big wave of heaviness hit me – right in the stomach. Those words ran deep for me – this came out of nowhere; I wasn't expecting it. My mind was racing, recalling recent events which were so contrary to what I'd just heard.

I got off the telephone extremely upset, but mainly confused. I just couldn't understand it all – it seemed so odd to me, all these mixed signals. A month ago this person was telling me I was so special to him, he had never been in love like this before, I would make an amazing mother to his children and he would look after me forever. He had given me so many signs and signals that we may get back together, but now I was recalling all the past conversations in my head. Was I imagining this? Was this just me reading way too much into things?

I couldn't understand how it could go from so hot to so cold without anything tragic happening in our relationship. I had never felt so broken in my life. What's worse, I just couldn't understand why or where it went wrong. I longed for it to be like it was when we first met. We had something so special. I felt no one had ever understood me in that way and it felt like such a deep connection.

Then I began to remember some of the things I had lived by and was taught, especially the knowledge of Twin Flames. If we were following the Twin Flame narrative, this is exactly what was supposed to happen! *I'm supposed to learn from this and work through it. This is just indicating that there is something in me that needs healing. It's an illusion that I need someone else, and so this is just part of the process of me becoming whole.* This was the time to clear the wound and come back into my power. I had already been 'doing the work' the entire way through the relationship and since we split, but now I recognised this as the separation stage; this was when perhaps healing work was required.

It was time for me to do some work, and by this point, clearing my 'blocks' or, simply put, releasing emotion or past pain was something I felt I could do as commonly as cook. It wasn't just a part of my life: it had become my life. The house was free for the entire day, so I decided to set up the area to really delve into this issue. Today needed to be deep, so I decided to opt for the Kali deck. For me, this was a special deck as the initiation (ritual into the teachings) healings and shifts I had received from this deck previously had *seemed* very helpful. If I worked with Kali, I meant business, because she was renowned for upheaval and removal of anything that doesn't serve us – even if this brought temporary upset and pain. I didn't realise at the time I was working with demonic energy.

The Last Card

I placed a pillow in front of the low table in front of me and made myself comfortable, I lit some sage, set up my protection for the area and set my intentions for the session. I shuffled the deck asking the question, "What is this situation with Toni showing me?" I pulled the first card and did some work, which led to a slight release of emotion. I felt there was more and I needed to go deeper.

Then came the precise moment that has never left me. I stretched out my hand to pick another card off the top of the deck and then I heard that same voice that I heard that day as I sat on my yoga mat. It was like this voice breathed into my being, "Are you sure you want to keep doing this to yourself?" My arm immediately froze. I remember just staring down at the deck with a million thoughts racing through my mind, the smoke of the burning sage gliding around my arm. Time just stopped and my heartbeat grew louder.

In this paused state, it's like I observed where I was and what my life had become. At this point, my hand had a slight grip on the top card, and I fought with my mind whether to pull the card or let go. Did I want to keep doing this to myself? The answer was no. I pulled my hand away from the deck and then broke down in tears. What I didn't realise is that act was more than just pulling away from a deck of cards: it was pulling away from all the false constructs I had built in and around my life. The show was over and it was time to stop pretending everything was ok.

There was so much that wasn't right with how I was living my life. I finally let go off the reins. It was the first time I was willing to look outside of the false light bubble I had been living in. Of course, letting go of the fantasy was hard. I enjoyed the fantasy and I wanted to hold onto it at all costs, even though it had been affecting my emotional, mental and physical wellbeing (by now, I was extremely thin) – but it was still more comforting than facing the cracks. Things had not been right with Toni for weeks and I was trying every healing modality to resolve what was going on inside – to clear, to ascend and become whole or just clear the blocks between us.

But it wasn't just since Toni. Over the past few years the amount of healing I did was simply not healthy; it was rare I wasn't working through some type of trauma, though, admittedly, not all of that was 'coming up' in triggers. Some of it I went looking for as I was so keen on accelerating to 5D and knew that anything of a lower vibration was just holding me back. It had become normal for me to be journeying somewhere, healing, upgrading, downloading or clearing something. For example, it may be one week I'd be working through abandonment and weeks later I'd be doing work around self love. All would involve recalling childhood events, past lives or the like, so called events that we are encouraged to view as traumatic, even though in reality the majority are not.

Weeks before this moment occurred, I was in a session with a coach, Emma, where she mentioned that she suspected I may be in a narcissistic relationship. At the time I instantly rejected this information, one, because I believed that labels were toxic, and two, because I thought she was vibrating on a lower level of consciousness than me and didn't understand the twin flame concept. However, after that call with her, there must have been some doubt about my convictions as I remember saying, "God, please show me the truth". So, after my tears had passed, I found myself reflecting on that conversation, and it became so clear that it had planted a seed. I knew it was time to revisit what Emma had said even though it was painful to even consider. The thing I was so offended by was now becoming clear. *Perhaps this was something I should be considering. Perhaps this relationship does have the potential to be something I am not fully aware of.*

What I did know is things just didn't match up – something was not quite right. I jumped on a call with Emma and, as we spoke, my jaw dropped. She walked me through the basic dynamics of a covert narcissistic relationship. It was like she was describing my entire relationship with Toni. I felt numb and in shock. I had never looked into the topic of narcissism before. I merely saw anyone not acting out of love as simply being in pain and I would have compassion for them. It really opened my eyes to my naivety, as I always took people at face value. I had learnt to identify people who do good things as good people, people who say nice things as nice people – all very straightforward. But this really opened my eyes to the fact that darkness is calculated. It comes as your friend, and can package itself in whatever you desire the most. I had been single seven years prior to Toni and there were times when I really liked the idea of having a partner and for someone to come into my life who understood me. So he became that person intentionally.

Regardless of my dislike of labels, I've come to realise that they are sometimes necessary. There are mental, emotional, and psychological issues and there needs to be some way of defining them so we can identify, acknowledge and accept the behaviours, then understand and process them. We cannot overcome anything by remaining ignorant of it. It was not like following New Age thought, where I was taught I could simply reject something from my reality. I've learnt that doesn't mean the objective reality is not there: that remains. What it means was I wasn't accepting it and would remain ignorant of it for as long as I choose to. I no longer wanted to remain ignorant. I wanted the truth above all else, so I decided to research narcissism. I was shocked by what I found. As the Bible says, "... and you will know the truth, and the truth will set you free".

"A man who flatters his neighbour spreads a net for his feet."

Proverbs 29:5

The Dynamics of Narcissism

B efore we start, I will point out I'm no expert on narcissism, but this is just what I've learnt. However, when we research the information below, the following dynamics seem to be very consistent in the reports of secular professionals in this area. So let's take a closer look into the dynamics of a narcissistic relationship. I found it consists of three main stages.

Stage 1 - The Idealisation Stage (nicknamed the Love Bomb)

The Idealisation stage is basically the start of the relationship. It's a stage where the narcissist will shower the other person with love, attention, and affection to a high degree. They will get to know us as a person and what we long for, and they will become that thing. This feels amazing, just like a whirlwind romance, being swept off our feet. I remember using that expression during this phase: we feel we've finally met someone who captivates us and is head over heels in love with us.

The words 'soul mate' and 'twin flame' will likely be used a lot. In my case I was well into this thinking already, and felt I had a soul connection with a lot of people around me from past lives. Things like "I've always dreamt of someone as perfect as you" or similar may be used. They almost worship you in a way, give you so much praise and time that you just feel on top of the world. Big gestures are proffered especially in material form to show their love for you. It's overwhelming the things they say and do that are so flattering. Imagine someone who could adore us that much! Such an outpouring of attention, everything you've ever longed to hear and feel! I felt so overwhelmed by just how crazily in love this person was with me that I convinced myself I felt the same too. Because we are on such a high, we mistake it for love. We think this person just makes us feel on top of the world when we are with them and so this means we are meant to be together; but in reality, we are just reacting to the over showering of attention and affection.

Now you may be thinking some of these things are common in a healthy relationship to a certain degree (minus the twin flame) when people like each other. But the main difference in a narcissistic relationship is it's very intense, and very quick. It's extreme, and many of us who come out of this type of manipulation always admit after that the pace of the relationship did bring up red flags. But we tended to dismiss them because we were being love bombed, and enjoyed this liaison way too much. We are told "I love you" typically in a matter of weeks. It feels too soon – doesn't feel right – but we move on with it anyway because we are blinded by the showering of love and then convince ourselves we feel the same. What we don't see going on underneath the surface of the relationship is the degree of manipulation of feelings, emotions, fears, and desires.

Normally, the attention comes with some type of security offered, so if you've experienced any kind of abandonment in your life, the promise will be "I'll never leave you". If you're struggling with paying bills, it's maybe "I promise I will always look after you and I'm here to take care of you". This can play on our insecurities, needs and desires along with our emotional trauma. They come as our saviour. Satan mimics everything about Jesus, even coming as Saviour. You can see why this is nicknamed 'the love bomb', as it's a mass explosion of affection and attention that comes out of nowhere. You feel as though the planets are aligned, and you're finally receiving the love you deserve sent from the universe!! As we experience such heightened sensations and emotions during this period, our flesh gets lit.

However, in reality, we're entering into a fantasy, driven by emotion and euphoria. We're moving so quickly, we don't have time to stop and think about things logically. But this is the whole illusion that's created. During the love bomb, the narcissist will future fake, so they paint a picture of your future together, perhaps where you'll live, where you'll go on holiday, things you will do together.

Every relationship is different, but this is where the damage is really done; this is where the bonds are formed. Now the love bomb stage normally doesn't last long – roughly three to six months. This is also why people don't need to be in a relationship with a narcissist for long to experience the damaging effects as all the damage is done in the first few months of the relationship.

So how is this connected to twin flame relationships? Well, the love bomb stage is often disguised as the intense twin flame reunion. We are charmed, flattered with obvious chemistry with a complete rush of emotion, adrenaline, and infatuation, so we perceive this as some divine meeting orchestrated by the universe. It seems like every wrong past relationship was completely right as it's led you to this person. The feeling of euphoria and attraction is beyond normal. We think to ourselves, *This person must be my twin flame as I've never felt like this before.* Likely spirit would also have been sending 'confirmation' messages at this point.

Stage 2 - The Devaluing Stage

Now, sadly, this is when the love bubble begins to defuse. Now the upsetting truth sinks in. During the love bomb stage, the narcissist has come to know your weaknesses, your insecurities and your needs and wants. They have showered you with so much attention and praise you could almost burst, so now they start to take that away. Yes, it pains me to say this but they build you up, to intentionally pull you back down – and it works! It's likely been months of intense time spent together – texts, phone calls, gifts – and now that's going to change. They begin to withdraw love, attention, and affection, and if you question this, you'll likely be accused of being needy, sensitive, or making a big deal out of nothing. This is where the cracks in the relationship start to appear, although this is also where our cognitive dissonance plays a big part.

Since we have already decided that this person loves us, they want the best for us and their intentions are pure, we are completely blinded by the showering of affection we receive during the love bomb phase. *My mind is made up by this point; we're crazy about each other and meant to be together*, we think. Obviously for someone to treat us in such a way, with such grand gestures and open displays of affection, we don't doubt this person is in love. This makes the devaluing stage very hard to nail for what it really is: a form of emotional and mental abuse. We are so completely blinded by the love bomb that our guard is completely down to anything with impure motives.

There may have been many warning signs popping up along the way, but due to the blinding of the love bomb, we disregard them, pass them off as something else and even make excuses for the person. We do everything to remain in the fantasy that it's real. This is where we are devalued, degraded, put down, and the love and affection we were once showered with is taken away from us. Gas lighting and projection now enter the relationship. Every time you pull them up on their behaviour, you will be accused of being crazy, over-sensitive, insecure, or just causing problems over silly things, and it will always be your fault. In fact, the only time they will admit blame is when you decide to leave, or look like you might: a narcissist does not like to be dumped.

So let's take a look closer at some of the factors at play in the devaluation stage:

Gaslighting - this phrase become popular from a psychological thriller film (Gaslight 1944) about a husband who was deliberately dimming the gaslights to lead his wife into believe she was going insane. It's a form of abuse where another person will repeatedly cause you to question your own sanity, perception of reality and memory. They do this deliberately and knowingly going against truth.

When this is done, it's normally done with such conviction that it's hard not to believe. It seems that when people say things with such confidence and certainty, it must be believable. You think to yourself, *It must be true,* or *I don't think they would react in such a way.* Then you begin to question whether you misinterpreted a situation or event. This is damaging as what begins to happen is we start to lose confidence in ourselves and our own judgement. In effect, we lose trust in ourselves.

People who have experienced this type of abuse for some time can sometime become so dependent on the thoughts and words of people around them that they look to others to define life for them. One example of a gas light could be this: your partner makes an obviously flirtatious remark to a girl on social media. When you express how this made you feel uncomfortable, they can fly off the handle and the next thing you know, they're discussing your controlling nature. It always goes back to you being the problem. The conversation will likely end up about how you need help with trust issues, and perhaps professional help. The original issue is no longer the point of discussion: you and your issue are.

Degrading - this is simply putting you down and is likely to happen through playing on your insecurities, which they will be fully aware of by now because you told them. This is something for which they would have gone out their way to make you feel secure about during the love bomb; however, the tables are now turned. They will highlight these insecurities randomly. For example, it may be your dress sense they comment on as you go out the door, "Is that what you are wearing?" Then when you respond "Yes," they remain silent. This is something you're already insecure about, and they know it. They intentionally haven't responded to you, only implying they think it doesn't look good, so now that plays on your mind and lowers your confidence.

Again, where the narcissist used to give you so much love and affection, now they regularly act uninterested and detached. They speak through silence and often ignore you completely. You can sit there telling the narcissist something really important to you, spilling your heart out almost, or sharing something you are really excited about, and they will not give any type of response. Sometimes they may even change the subject entirely. This is devaluing what you're saying. It sends the message you are unimportant; they just do not value you or the conversation. This is a huge contrast to the love bomb stage where they were attentive to every word. This change from hot to cold builds up further insecurity and confusion. We could possibly start rethinking the conversation, second guessing ourselves, or replaying it in our heads fearing we said something silly or offensive to the other person.

The degrading stage in a twin flame relationship is disguised as the 'triggering stage' where apparently you show each other aspects of yourself that need healing. In reality it is devaluation and a form of abuse. That's why there's always one who's saying, "He/She isn't doing the work", and because they aren't, they are not able to access that type of emotion. It's common for a narcissist to be in healing sessions or new age practices and never have any emotional experience like the rest of us; this is because they are shut off from it. They cannot heal, simply because they will not accept anything that 'needs work'.

This stage is so unhealthy and will likely start to affect our physical body too as many lose weight during the devaluation stage. No wonder so many are caught up in the intense cycle of a twin flame relationship, not realising it's abuse disguised as spiritual development, which makes you believe it's best to continue the path, and even be convinced it's for the higher good of the planet.

Stage 3 - The Discarding Stage

The discard phase hurts. By the time we get to this point the relationship would have been going downhill for some time, and the narcissist has been constructing this the entire time. The victim would have been doing everything in their power to restore the relationship to where it was in the beginning – the love bomb stage –while the narcissist has been moving further away, though still giving pockets of hope. This is known as 'bread crumbing'. When things are not going well, one breadcrumb planted in a sentence can give false hope to keep us trying to resolve the relationship. They could say something like, "I know we are taking some time apart, but we never know what the future holds and I do miss you."

But trying to make things work with a narcissist is like swimming upstream in the roughest of waters; it's fighting a losing battle. During the devaluation stage the narcissist has started to reject you. Since they require constant admiration, during the last stage they would have seeking that elsewhere; they need some form of energy supply from someone, always. Once they have another supply in the picture to go into the love bomb stage, this is when you will be discarded. If a narcissist breaks if off with you officially, then that means they have found another supply for sure; that's the only way they will move on. This is usually another romance, though it could be a friend or companion as well.

Now, there never really is a full discard, for they may block you here and there to intentionally affect you. It is very well known that the narcissist will never fully cut ties. There are a few reasons for this, the main one being, they may need you as back-up in the future, so when things don't work out with the new prospect, they may come back into your life and walk through the cycle once more. You'll go back to the love bomb stage and then it will naturally take its course again from there. This is how some end up in a kind of mix of love bomb, degrade and discard – a mixed stew to put it mildly.

Sadly, one of the reasons the narcissist wants to maintain some type of relationship is simply that they still want some type of supply from you. This emotional fuel is going to come from your reaction to their new relationship. They still want to be in control and have a hold of your life and they now do this out of your hurt. Remember the future faking? The things they promised you and said you'll share together? It is common for them to give everything you wanted and desired for the future to the new supply. This can really hurt. He promised you would go to Paris one day – you'll see them both tagged in at the airport to go on the trip he promised you. Wanted a certain piece of jewellery? Guess what; she's getting it! It's crazy but so true! Sadly, the narcissist does this because, even when you're not together, they still want to have a hold over your life. They do it for the impact it will have on you. If they know it has affected you, that's perfect. These people want overall control of you and your emotions, which is the underlying theme in all deceptions.

In the twin flame relationship, the discard is technically the separation. Now in a narcissistic relationship the trauma bond (neurological pathway dopamine) has already been made, so during the separation the abused (victim), if they think they are in a twin flame relationship, will be desperately seeking a reunion. The twin flame narrative is satanic without question, keeping you in cycles of abuse and control and making you believe it's all for a great cause – it's deception at its darkest.

By contrast, God works in seasons, where there are times of hardship, excitement, promotion, challenges, and testing; but you're always evolving in a healthy way, and you walk through your trials differently. However, during twin flame separation, it's so common to seek tarot readers, psychics, and mediums, with the hope of them comforting us with some kind of sign that the partner is going to come back. It's the enemy's web of lies that just keeps us trapped and going round in circles. I used to put my faith in the 'spirits' and the divine guidance I was receiving ... but little did I know this was just the start of the domino effect of truths ready to tumble my way.

Please know that I understand this is hard to comprehend when evaluating New Age teaching. We are taught everyone is love. But the reality is that it's just not so and this is not some dreamt up spiritual narrative. Narcissism is a clinically diagnosed psychological condition and there is ample evidence that a large number of such people exist. In an ideal world, it wouldn't be this way, but in a hard world it is the truth and one that I found hard to swallow. The New Age had conditioned me into believing that, if I said anything remotely unkind about someone else, even if it was true, then I was not a nice person. Or I was just harbouring some anger or hate inside and I needed to go work on myself. I know how some people may view what I'm saying as mean and unloving – I once reacted in exactly the same way. It took some time for me to come to terms with the fact that people can be intentionally manipulative. It's a hard truth, but now I'm Christian, I see this as the enemy working through people: they just don't know it. Satan has a hold of them in so many ways and I pray they are set free from his grip. I don't believe it's the people; I believe it's the spirits that are working through them. I take no enjoyment from sharing this at all, but the fact, is by denying these truths – and they are truths – then I'm denying my and many other people's experiences with narcissistic abuse. There is freedom from this, but without acknowledging the issue, the freedom will remain unobtainable.

One thing I do also want to highlight is that 'narcissism' has become a bit of a buzz word of the late, one, because it's being uncovered, but two, because of social media. I want to share this in the correct understanding and context because we all do have narcissistic traits and tendencies. So I'm not referring to just ways in which the world rubs off on us – we all can do things that are narcissistic according to what we were taught, or shown. I'm not referring to this when I refer to narcissism; I'm referring to full blown Narcissistic Personality Disorder which is a clinically diagnosed mental health condition, and to expand on that, the term 'covert narcissism'.

There are still parts of me that still hate this kind of talk, because I simply dislike saying such things about people. But – whether I like saying it or not – doesn't change the fact it's true and widespread in the world today. The world is run on narcissism, and a large part of that stems from pride. The New Age is so prideful because we build ourselves up and not God, we promote us and not God, we exalt ourselves and not God. It's all about puffing ourselves up. This is how manipulation works. It comes, not just as your friend, but your best friend with a rainbow and glitter. It comes as an instant answer to all your problems, as the Bible says, "Even Satan himself pretends to be an angel of light". This is how people are deceived: satan comes as light ... that's how he comes into your life ... as your saviour... **he mimics** everything that Jesus is.

I have respect for anyone who's been through a narcissistic relationship just because I know the hell you have walked through. I don't think I've ever felt so much pain in all my life. It ran deep and it hurt badly; but this also led me to the true light, which I'm so grateful for.

See, in the New Age I would have been pointing people to the 'light'. I would have told them that it's just someone in pain, but I was so ignorant of what really goes on in the world. Some people have experienced year upon year of abuse, hurt and pain from narcissistic abuse. We are dealing with people who are unable to feel empathy or compassion for people. Not that they choose not to but they can't. This is the heart-breaking thing; they are unable to relate to others in a normal way.

So, what happens when we reject a narcissist? Normally, we would have to discover the relationship is abusive in order to leave: usually the intention is to seek to destroy. From their point of view, no one can leave them. They can retaliate by bringing about a smear campaign, and there will be lies spread about you, or fabricated versions or half-truths. They will seek to destroy your reputation by any means possible. They want to destroy you as a person and how everyone perceives you. Thankfully, my relationship ended with me being discarded and I knew it was time to go with no contact. I don't know anything about what was said about me, as I blocked him and his friends for the sake of being fully free from the relationship. But I'm sure things would have been said as it's part of their personality. The only way to be fully free is to have no contact. This also made me realise that we can't believe rumours and gossip and shouldn't entertain them as the Bible tells us.

With hindsight, I can't help but feel silly for falling for it all. Looking back at the love bomb, there were so many times where I knew things didn't feel right. The tell-tale signs were there; I just chose to not see them. Interesting how we do that when we don't want to face the truths, just as Jesus' hand of grace is continuously held out, but we choose to reject the notion of sin and go about our lives.

Sometimes I wonder, if the wheels hadn't fallen off in that relationship, whether I would ever have been able to see past my pride to receive the message of the Gospel. I'm thankful for that relationship in so many ways because, as much as it was emotional abuse, it led me to Christ. I do share some deep reflections on this topic in a later chapter, but for now, I want to say that, through the strength of Jesus Christ, I've come to a place where I've forgiven Toni. I pray for God to change his heart, just like He did mine. For as long as God puts this on my heart, Toni will remain in my prayers.

"Now the Spirit expressly says that in later times some will depart from the faith by devoting themselves to deceitful spirits and teachings of demons"

1 Timothy 4:1

False Light

During the break-up phase of the relationship, information kept coming into my space about false light. At first, I thought I had figured out what the false light was – it was the corrupt spirituality of the mainstream media. But now I was starting to come across more deceptions.

As more information kept coming to me, some of the revelations started to feel uncomfortably personal, as they related to some of the things I practised myself. In the past, I would have instantly dismissed many of the claims and always had some sort of belief to support this. But now I realised I'd been so blinded by Toni, alarm bells were immediately going off in my head with my 'spirit guides' and 'messages of spirit' I had received. For one thing, I couldn't understand how I was in a toxic, unhealthy, narcissistic relationship and my guides could be encouraging it the entire way through. I remember occasions when I was being gaslit that 'spirit' was telling me I needed to clear my blocks, heal, and look within. How can my guides that supposedly love me unconditionally want me to stay in an abusive relationship? They encouraged the relationship and even got me excited by it. No matter how I looked at it, I just couldn't justify the guidance I had received.

I remember seeing a psychic two weeks before Toni and I broke up. She said some accurate things which gained my trust; and then she continued to share that Toni was my soul mate, that we would move in together and have a healing business together. This couldn't have been further from the truth, but what reaction did this have on me? It sucked me into the fantasy even more, and opened me to more delusion. This is Satan's hook – tell you want you want to hear, and keep you in the cycle. Every time doubt creeps in, feed you with more consoling lies. The issue is we choose to believe things much more easily when it matches our desires. Sadly, even when they are lies, they are still comforting. All this wasn't adding up, and I stopped my regular practices as well as interacting with spirit. My thinking was I just needed to find out what was going on before I went any further. One thing I knew for sure there was something was 'off', and this led me to dig deeper into the claim of false light deception.

There were so many events and conversations that happened leading to my salvation that sometimes I even get confused about the timeline and order of exactly what happened. I recall conversations from even a year earlier about false light, which at the time seemed so silly. But I can see how these little moments were slowly chipping away at the lies. Somehow, I started connecting with people who talked openly about false light, many of them preaching Jesus as the Way. I met a friend, Emily, through speaking out about what

I was discovering online. She had been going through a similar pattern. She was very straight talking and a new believer in Christ. She encouraged me to read the Bible and get to know Jesus myself. Coincidently (or not so) months before all this, during a visit to my nan, I noticed she had a Bible on her book shelf and, knowing my nan was an atheist, I asked to have it. Unsurprisingly, she was happy to let it go. I was thinking to myself, *I'd like to know what's in that book to make people so trapped in religion.* My plan was to use this for research. This is just evidence that God can use all things for His glory; He used my pride to give me a bible.

What the Bible Says about Channelling

I began to read, and this was when I was shocked to discover the following. In the Bible, God tells us not to go to mediums, or dabble with witchcraft and the like. Leviticus 19:31: "Do not turn to mediums or necromancers, do not seek them out and so make yourselves unclean by them; I am the Lord your God." Suddenly I started to realise why my 'spirit guides' had encouraged me to enter and continue the relationship with Toni: they didn't love me unconditionally; they were deceptive.

I think most people who subscribe to the concept of twin flame relationships may have sought out mediums and readings; it's part of the hook to keep you trapped in the cycle. In the book of Deuteronomy 18:10-12, "Anyone who practices divination or tells fortunes or interprets omens, or a sorcerer or a charmer or a medium or a necromancer or one who inquires of the dead, for whoever does these things is an abomination to the Lord." These very things that God commands us not to do, we're receiving as our 'divine guidance'. Now this was not easy for me to accept or hear, and if it wasn't for my experience with Toni, then I wonder if I would have ever seen into the deceit. I had gone down so many avenues before accepting the truth. I wondered if perhaps it was just a particular energy I was working with. But at the time I couldn't understand that as all the programs I was channelling and guidance I was receiving appeared to be the best they'd ever been.

I know most of those who disbelieve what I say will opt for the reaction, "Well, she obviously didn't discern the spirits well," or "Sounds like she just has an entity attachment". But I was so thorough in that area. I always had good intentions, and set the intention with very direct and precise language, and called in my means of protection. This progressed throughout my journey of how I would do this and what energy I would choose to call in. All this was never overlooked. I've now come to realise, the whole energy protection thing is just something that is there to lead you into a false sense of security. It's to build our confidence, to make us think and feel we are in control and know exactly what we are doing. If, in the New Age the spirits are demonic or deceptive spirits, then all the advice on how to discern them is channelled from the same spirits, and therefore would be lies. There is a reason why God says in the Bible not to go into these realms. How can the spirits be trusted when Jesus calls Satan the father of lies? (John 8:44)

There was one method I was told to use whenever 'an energy' came into my space. I was to ask the energy if it loves me unconditionally three times. Now, this is twisted counsel, like everything else. The Bible tells us to test the spirits, referring to the spirits which influence people, to test whether they are speaking from the Holy Spirit or the antichrist as their source. Anyhow, I remember using this method and believing that apparently spirits can't lie three times. This does seem a little silly now but at the time I saw it as being discerning. I was taught it's about my intention; when entering in the energy session my intention was the key and narrative to the session. Again, this just adds to the false sense of security, like we are in control of what's happening.

The best way to manipulate people and lead them astray is to make them feel like they have got there all by themselves. It's far easier to move people in a certain direction if you convince them it's for the highest good –for themselves and humanity, and that they have made the choices and decisions, when really in the New Age it's our experiences that are determining the next steps and actions.

There were many times I asked these spirits if they loved me unconditionally three times. Some did say no on the last question. Some even morphed into 'dark' energy. They would leave and then another spirit would come in and I'd ask again and this one would answer yes all three times. Bingo! That wasn't hard to get me to engage, was it? Not only that, but now I would feel super confident that I was working with good energy and that I was able to discern spirits well. What a false road to go down – all smoke and mirrors!

I'm sure many reading this book would know what channelling is, but for those who do not, I shall provide a short overview. Channelling is basically allowing a spirit to use us as a channel for spiritual information to be shared with others. I used to channel certain energies and deities in energy sessions. Now I don't mean that they would take over my body like a medium in a trance, but more that they were using me as a portal for knowledge to pass through. So the information wasn't coming from me; it was coming from them. Now there is no way of knowing if channelled material is the truth or not, unless it 'resonates' with the receiver. But knowing that its source is demonic and that the devil is a liar, how can anyone put their trust in it? Asking someone if a message resonates is just like saying, "Do you like this message? If not, we can just pretend spirit didn't say it". The prophets in the Bible were never there to deliver ear tickling messages, and they certainly wouldn't have asked anyone if it resonated. Just imagine, "You're a sinner and the Lord said to repent and turn from your sin. Does this resonate?"

This pretty much is how I did every guided meditation. I would be shown where to go and what to do, and I would have my methods of discernment to check along the way. I never claimed to speak to dead people, although there have been one or two occasions when that kind of energy did appear. However, I was never open to or interested in knowing that much – I saw it as too 3D spiritually. The Starseed narrative really gets you up there: it makes you feel you're ahead of others, on the cusp of the new earth. I was only interested in working with higher vibrations such as ascended masters.

But it's just the same thing that's always been there, only they use different words to make it sound new and exciting. Instead of 'guidance', it's 'download'; instead of 'healing', it's 'upgrade'. They now use words like 'transmission', 'activation', 'integrate', 'code', which is all basically prepping for the big AI agendas at play. I've found how many of these deceptive spirits operate: they flatter, they puff us up, make us feel special or predict things that will delight us with excitement. They are actually rather narcissistic, and completely love bomb. Once we have a reading or a reiki session, we can feel on a high and elated plane. Until then, we are triggered and need to raise our vibration again, so off we go again to the healing practitioner. It's in constant cycles, and the energy can be oppressive – I was once stuck in a spiral of spiritual abuse with the energy that was attached to me. Channelling has been the route of many New Age theories and teachings. There is a famous channeller who channels an entity with a well known biblical name – which makes it all the more deceptive. Apparently this entity wouldn't leave her alone until she decided to work with it and then channelled a book that takes scripture and twists it.

I don't know the exact technical term – whether it's demons, fallen angels or lying spirits – but I have no doubt that whatever these people are channelling is not leading us to truth. They come bearing gifts for humanity, secret knowledge, and understanding, but their main intention is to pull people away from the Bible. All this is done in the name of 'love'. The New Age is happy to talk about Jesus as a prophet and healer but, as with any deception, anything goes except the Cross. For a believer, the works of our salvation always lead back to the Cross. That's where our gift of grace is found – at the cross – and any distortion of the truth is always an attack on the cross. Satan doesn't care if you love Jesus as long as you don't believe He died for your sins on the cross, was buried and rose again three days later. That's what makes someone a Christian: believing in the gospel.

Many people have brought up to me the claim that the Bible was written by the Holy Spirit. They argue that, since this too channelled, how can you say one is deceptive and the other is not? Yes, the Bible was written by the Holy Spirit in that He inspired different writers to write the various books of the Bible. The Bible makes mention of many other spirits; but there is only one Spirit that is of God, and that is the Holy Spirit. Jesus talks about the Holy Spirit as a helper; He says that the helper should always be pointing people to Him. And that's what the Holy Spirit does. The Holy Spirit is not something we 'channel'; the Holy Spirit is **dwells within us** when we receive Him. The Holy Spirit is a Person and part of the triune God. If He is a person who lives inside of us, why is this different from other spirits living inside of us? Because the other spirits are not of God and their nature is contrary to the things of God. You'll notice the other spirits will entice us to sin in some way, most likely through our sexual passions, greedy desires and selfish ambition.

But really, it isn't about me just sharing how these spirits are false light. There's no point highlighting the lies if we do not have any truth as a basis of comparison, so my job in this book is to point you to the truth: Jesus. Only when we get to know Jesus – what He said, what He did and what He preached – only then can we see into the lies more clearly.

Jesus was only concerned with one Spirit in the Bible, the Holy Spirit. Any other spirit He cast out from people. He said the Holy Spirit would direct people to Him. Why would He say that? Because of His work of redemption. So, we know whether a spirit is from God based on whether it leads people to Christ, the true Christ of the Bible. This is why the Bible says to "test the spirits". Test the spirits of prophets or teachers to determine whether they are leading people to the truth – Jesus Christ who came in the flesh as man – not a distortion of Christ such as an avatar, Ascended Master or just a type of 'consciousness'.

"And you also were included in Christ when you heard the message of truth, the gospel of your salvation. When you believed, you were marked in him with a seal, the promised Holy Spirit" (Ephesians 1:13-14).

We don't need to 'call in' energy; we don't need to vibrate on a certain frequency; we don't need to pay someone for an attunement to receive the Holy Spirit.

We simply receive the Holy Spirit by believing, in Jesus and the works He did for us.

"And this is my prayer: that your love may abound more and more in knowledge and depth of insight, so that you may be able to discern what is best and may be pure and blameless for the day of Christ"

Philippians 1:9-10

Experiences & Discernment

E xperience and feeling was once the way for me to discern
all things and make decisions. I always used to think, *Sure,
people say I'm crazy thinking I'm a Starseed, but they haven't experienced what I have* or *They are just not awake.* I've come to learn
that, when we make decisions based solely on personal experience,
we will certainly be led down some dark roads, as we know spirits
lie – very convincingly at that.

I had what I believed to be genuine experiences with Star Beings, Goddesses and Ascended Masters. They made everything
seem so real and believable. I was completely sold. Everyone's path
is different. Some take a while to come to the belief they are a
Starseed, some just believe when they hear it, but most are convinced through an experience. Most experiences I think would
be like mine, in stages: at first the concept seems farfetched; then
'spirit' would lead you to people online, or books or oracle decks

that lead you to believe this phenomenon actually exists. Then a personal experience would happen and a full conversion takes place. So how do I now see these experiences?

Spirits have the power to massively manipulate the target. First, they know you, they know what you want to hear, they know what makes you emotional, they know what to say to get you to where they want. They can influence your feelings with sensations, encouraging words, and messages. But what if we were being encouraged towards destruction and lies? Would we know it if they got us thinking it's all a good idea? The spirits have done such a good job of emotional, mental, and spiritual manipulation, because they have earned the victim's trust and have persuaded them that it's all good. The most successful form of control is when you have people willingly participating.

When I look at how I was living, I was in the mindset it was a good thing that I was being triggered left, right, and centre and needed to heal. It was a good idea I cut ties with friends because they drained my energy and remained in 3D. It was a good idea to pay people to tell me that my twin flame was going to work out to give me a glimmer of hope. It was a good idea I was getting in debt having to pay thousands for programs I couldn't afford. It was a good idea I detached myself more and more from reality because I was too cosmic. It was a good idea I had my boundaries up to people whom I should have been there for. It was a good idea I ignored the larger issues of the world because I was focusing on positivity. It was a good idea I was putting myself first because I deserved it – you've got to love yourself, right?! This was all for the good of me, the planet and the coming of the New Age. How blinkered can you get!

So discovering the truth about these spirits did bring some confusion because it ran counter to my own experiences. In some sessions, I felt such love and peace that I struggled to see how those feelings could be false. I prayed on this and can now see two things clearly here. Feelings are always real, but it doesn't necessarily mean the things (the situation / our perception) that caused the feelings are. Sadly, we can be very easily manipulated, and our feelings are certainly not a true reflection of what's going on. We can easily see this demonstrated in the things children cry about because sometimes it hard to even understand why a child is crying. They see things in their reality that are just not there; they don't see the world through mature eyes. Well, that doesn't stop when we are adult. Imagine how different we would be if we could see the world with God's eyes, when we follow Jesus, and He begins to share that with you.

I do also hold the view that some occasions could well have genuinely been an experience with the One True Living God. We can have an experience with God – anyone can. But there's a difference between having an experience with God and having a relationship with God. God can meet us anywhere, anytime, if He chooses to. But, in terms of a deep relationship with Him, He has offered the gift of salvation in Christ for that, which is up to us to accept if we choose. God isn't forcing us into relationship or to love Him.

He has given us the way of freedom through Christ. What are you choosing?

Out of all the experiences, the most challenging thing for me to accept was the idea of past life experiences. I had been through so many, and at the time believed I had truly travelled through space and time to revisit these lives, calling back gifts, clearing past life wounds and the like. I even had a past life memory of me as a Starseed choosing to come to earth. In this particular session I was a leader and influenced my community to come to earth. I remember I could see that I chose to reconnect with my community in this life to lead them into discovering their true identity and their own divinity.

Spirit used to say things like "Remember who you are" and "You've been preparing for this for life times" – it was so tickling to the ear. They know how to get you and that got me. Now, this 'past life' experience came with so much emotion; I could remember being saddened by what I saw on earth. This is important to note as when we cry, we see this as a means of confirmation it's real. But think about this, when you watch a movie or hear a song that moves you to tears, does that mean it's real? No, of course not! It just means that it's tugged at your feelings and produced a reaction but you're not actually experiencing what's happening in the movie or song. This is how it's so easy to get sucked in to the New Age.

The number of times I heard people talk about energy sessions and they say, "It was so powerful, I cried" as confirmation it was the real deal! I've come to realise this is not a good basis for discernment because, whether we cry or not, that doesn't change the truth. Whether our feelings know the truth or not, reality still stands. Our feelings constantly change about people, situations, and a whole host of things, all in the space of seconds, too. We've all had that one past relationship that just didn't end well. Remember being in love with that ex? How do you feel about them now though?

This is how I feel about my past experiences in the New Age. At the time I was fanatically in love with those spirits, but now I can see them for what they are. The veil has been lifted and now I see them as demonic entities. Now I'm not saying we just disregard feeling and emotion altogether, but as the Bible states, the heart is deceitful: "The heart is deceitful above all things, and desperately wicked: who can know it?" (Jeremiah 17:9)

Therefore, feelings shouldn't dominate all our decision-making and means of discernment, as our feelings can be easily impacted by outside factors, events and simply our longing to feel good. If feelings were a compass to navigate life, as the New Age teaches that with all big decisions, follow the heart, follow pleasure, and follow what feels good, then we are bound to wind up in deception. I mean that's how I was so subjected to a love bomb – it all felt so good!

I remember when I first watched Marley & Me, I cried so much that if anyone were to walk in, they would have thought it was my dog that died. But was it? Was anything in that experience real? The only thing that was real was my emotion. *I did feel sad* and that feeling generated tears. But this event wasn't happening to me; I was just watching it on a screen. Therefore, the *cause* of my emotions wasn't real; but my emotions were real, because that's the feeling that was generated from watching. I felt like it was happening to me, but this was far from reality. What films and music are very good at doing is moving us into another state, and our imagination takes us elsewhere. We can imagine we are that person losing the dog, or we even think of our dog and what it would be like to lose it. This then takes us to a situation and, before you know it, you are emotionally experiencing something that isn't real.

Now if we can get like that over a film, why would we not think spirits can manipulate our feelings in the same way by moving us into another false reality? But this time we are not aware it's false: we truly think we are experiencing certain things in other dimensions. There are two theories that I have for what we experience. One is when we voluntarily go into trance and the other is an altered state similar to hypnotherapy, when we enter a dimension in which our imagination can take the lead. I always wonder what was imprinted in my subconscious as a child too as some of my 'past life' experiences reminded me of scenes from things I'd watched on TV as a kid. Mainly I believe it's spirits we open ourselves up to that project images on our minds. Now I see that every time I took part in an attunement, download, upgrade, or anything of the like, I was opening myself up to the demonic. I would come away more 'open' to spirit or more in touch with my 'gifts'.

I'm convinced that opening the third eye is opening ourselves up to demonic oppression. The third eye is believed to be a *chakra* or energy centre on the forehead apparently linked to intuition, vision (into spirit realms) and perception. Demonic spirits influence and, in more severe cases, control our minds and thoughts. I say influence or control as there are varying degrees of control just as being oppressed is not being possessed. I'm convinced a lot of it happens when we try and open our third eye or participate in attunements, where we open ourselves up to these spirits even more.

The New Age encourages us to champion emotion very early on in the journey. Everything is about how it makes us feel, how we have all these suppressed emotions and the key to our freedom is in expressing them. Emotions take the driver's seat in our life. So we operate according to: how does this person make you feel? How does it feel working with this coach? How does it feel saying no to this person? The issue is that emotions can be easily manipulated and change. On the other hand, the Bible says to make decisions using discernment and wisdom. This doesn't mean emotions are completely invalid, but they are meant to be a subordinate part of the decision, not the main indicator. Decisions made with wisdom are based on questioning whether we are seeing the situation clearly, what are our motives for participating and, more importantly, what are the consequences of our actions – how will they affect others and our relationship with God. We also pray for the Lord's counsel and for His will to be done in our decision making.

I am not dismissing emotions at all. Emotions can be a great indicator of what's going on, but the key point is that they relate to what's going on with **us**, and not necessarily what is ***actually happening in reality***. Ultimately, feelings are not the teacher of truth. I always think of the type of situations where we googled our symptoms when we felt ill, and next thing you know we are on the phone to our friend telling them we think we have some life-threatening disease and are considering driving down to the hospital for instant care. In reality, we have a common cold, but after google we've got four days to live!

God does and will continue to use 'supernatural' experiences with people. I've had some incredible encounters with the Father that I believe to be true. But I've also had some experiences that I thought were guidance from God, but later through reading my Bible and prayer, realised my misinterpretation of the situation. The closer I get to God, through prayer, relationship and reading my Bible, the more I get to know how He talks to me and through me and others by the power of the Holy Spirit.

The great pull in the Starseed deception is that it gives a sense of belonging and purpose; this is something we all crave. If we are searching for this and find it in the Starseed narrative, it can feel like the answer to it all. It plays on our desires and emotions from the get-go. It is in our nature to want to belong and be connected to something. I believe that every human being is endowed with a deep-down desire for connection with God. The Bible says "God has set eternity in the *human* heart" (Ecclesiastes 3:11). If that connection is missing or disrupted, it can leave us with the feeling of emptiness because of something missing in our lives. The Starseed narrative tries to rob us of that longing by giving another meaning to it. In the new age, whether we do it consciously or not, we are all searching.

I've come to know it's about finding the truth of not **what** we belong to, but **who** we belong to. It's not the earth, or the universe or light family. It's back with our **Maker**, a personal God who has gifted us with His Word so we can come to learn about Him. Walking with a personal God, one who wants to know me and I Him, has been so different from the new age. He has emotions, will and intellect too. The spirits I worked with in the new age were just controlling through flattery, "Do this, do that, and you're great!" But my God wants me to primarily know Him and His Son. I've found so much joy in knowing Jesus. With the spirits I worked with before, I would just ask for guidance and act upon it. But God shares His heart with me and wants to know mine. He walks with me through everything and uses my hardships to teach me endurance, to gain strength, and bring me closer to His Son.

The word of God, the Bible, is now at the centre of my faith. I remember when I first read Proverbs, all I kept thinking was, if only

I had all this knowledge when I was younger! Proverbs is one of the books in the wisdom literature, and when I first read it, it was like discovering treasure. When I make decisions now, I'm able to filter the emotion out of the situation. My fleshy desire is not the driving force behind my decisions because I know, if I follow the word of God, it will lead to the best place. My feelings can still be very much part of the decision process, but they're not the driver. Now that I've learnt to dismiss instant gratification and put off that temporary 'feel good' state, I've been able to make very sound decisions for the long-term concerning things that are real and long lasting.

Scripture is the best guide. It's God's word, and His guidance will challenge your worldly mindset once you start to develop that relationship with Him and hear Him speaking through His Word. "All scripture is breathed out by God and profitable for teaching, for reproof, for correction, and for training in righteousness" (2 Timothy 3:16). The thing is, we don't see what God sees; we don't know what God knows, for He is an all-knowing God. However, when we put our trust in Him and His word, and we follow that truth, even when our feelings dictate otherwise, we will certainly never regret it. I can trust God's word over my feelings and circumstances. I trust the Father loves me and is guiding me in the right direction even if I can't see where it leads.

As a believer, my new walk has been putting my faith in God completely. Choosing to trust implies that my view of the world is not how I always interpret it; but it is how God says it is. I can trust His eagle eye view, rather than my own positioning on the ground. I know my Maker cares for me deeply and I can surrender my will to Him and trust Him implicitly.

Proverbs 3:5-6: "Trust in the Lord with all your heart, and do not lean on your own understanding. In all your ways acknowledge him, and he will make straight your paths."

The Lord is true to His word.

"It is written in the Prophets: 'They will all be taught by God.' Everyone who has heard the Father and learned from him comes to me."

John 6:45

I Have Questions

It still took a process to fully receive Christ. I was certain though of the false light, I couldn't 'unsee' or 'unlearn' everything that had been revealed to me. At the same time, I was petrified of falling into another deception. Through studying the Bible, my walk with Christ was developing with the desire to know the word, to know the truth of who Christ is, and what He said and taught.

In the New Age I truly believed anyone who followed any type of religion was operating at a lower level of consciousness than me. For me, Christianity as low vibrational, antiquated belief system, a matrix where people are trapped. This was rather prideful of me but it's true. I was so wary of getting stuck somewhere like this and lowering my vibration. So it was a gradual process for me to unlearn a lot of the thinking I had adopted from the New Age. Our energy being at 'different levels' was one of them. This is quite ironic as the New Age really pushes the narrative of avoiding any type of division, but at the same time encourages you to feel more advanced than anyone who is unable to get on board with your beliefs. Apparently, they are behind or unable to understand due to their low vibration.

On the one hand, my heart was longing for Jesus as I just kept wanting to read about Him and learn about Him. On the other, I couldn't fully commit to going there because my vision was already fogged about Christianity from the New Age. *What if I was going into another deception?* I kept asking. The coming weeks I went into deep research and prayer for answers. I promised myself I wouldn't commit unless my logic, intellect, discernment, and heart were all singing from the same hymn sheet.

There were so many questions and God was so patient with me. I had my own personal reservations of why I could not accept the whole truth. These stemmed mainly from certain new age beliefs that clashed with Christianity. I will share some of them here.

False Belief One: No Such Thing as Sin

To most people, Christianity is the least appealing of faiths because of its concern with sin. When we think of becoming a Christian, we instantly think of limitations, rigid views, and being confined and restricted to rules. No one wakes up one day and is like, "Christianity looks really fun!" No, the message of the gospel is not typically music to our ears when we first hear it. It's common to have much resistance as the first thing we think of is the restrictions if we walk a Christian life. *I won't be able to do this or that as it's a sin.* The word 'sin' has such a stigma around it today, but it simply means to 'miss the mark' (think of an archer aiming at the target), when we deviate from the way in which God has instructed us to live. But the word of God says we are all sinners, even Christians, and the wages of sin is death (Romans 6.23). We are saved from that penalty because of our Saviour Jesus Christ.

So one of the first hurdles I had to get over was the concept of sin. How could a God so loving stop you from experiencing pleasure? How could a God be so controlling? Seriously! But it's like God gave me eyes to see and ears to hear: I was looking at things in this world, but I wasn't really seeing them until now. Even when I was in the new age, I believed this world was controlled by darker powers, but I never really noticed the links between all my pursuits. I knew that chart music, the movie industry and mainstream TV and advertising push certain agendas, but I never really noticed how much they push sin. It's everywhere – the place is drenched in sin – every lyric, every commercial; they're all just leading people into temptation. God hates adultery, drunkenness, theft, murder, lies, idolizing things or people, worship of other gods, fornication and all the things that society has come to love. All these values are advertised in the media on a constant basis.

So, instead of viewing God as this control freak, I wanted to understand why. I remember my own father telling me not to do such and such when I was younger. Of course, I didn't listen and chose to be the rebellious child; then I grew up and realised why he had warned me not to do those things. They were not good for me and would lead me down the wrong path: and they did. What if our heavenly Father is the same? What if this is for our own good? Let's looks at the fruits that sin produces and compare them with the fruit of following Jesus.

No fornication

Think of what would be avoided: abortion, broken hearts, divorce, sexual trauma, STDs – to name a few. What would materialize? More wholesome marriages as couple would have connected on a spiritual and emotional level prior to giving their body. You would be treating every date as a potential life partner, not as someone to sleep around with. Children actually grow up in a safe, stable family unit.

Now don't get me wrong. I'm not deluded enough to think all divorce would be totally eliminated or no one would ever be unfaithful to their spouse. At the end of the day, we do have a sinful nature, however we all must admit the figures would dramatically decrease.

Sobriety

Then there's the topic of sobriety, that is, remaining sober. Imagine a world without alcohol dependency! Think of the number of fights, casualties, thefts, mental health issues, suicides, addictions, broken homes and abuse that would have been avoided! By the way, some Christians like to claim getting intoxicated is fine as Jesus drank wine. However, the wine hadn't the same level of alcohol as it has today, or there were no chemicals that make you go wild for that matter. The Bible commands us to remain sober, so it's up to us to know our limits.

Now I don't think we need to go through every sin, but you see where I'm going with this. If much of sin has to do with dishonouring our fellow human being, won't the world be such a beautiful place without sin? Imagine a world where we followed Christ's commandments – ah, now we're talking! Love one another as yourself ... *er yes, please! I'd love to live in a world like this! I'm with You, Lord, Jesus Christ! I'm so with You!*

Now I look back and can't help but find it almost comical that I was so unaware I was drowning in a swamp of sin. Here was I trying to find my own way through the sludge and seeing smooth dry land right in front of me, then questioning if the land was real. We think it is saying no to freedom except that the dry land is actually the hand of Jesus, and it's being held out the entire time. We just never chose to see it or take notice of it, too busy trying to make ourselves 'happy' in the sludge! I've come to realise denying the existence of sin doesn't make it go away, but it does make the solution go away. How can we see the solution if we don't think there is a problem?

False Belief Two: Christians Are Trapped in an Old Paradigm

I used to think Christians needed some type of awakening to bring them out of their delusion. I never actually knew what they believed because I'd never read the Bible, but I just knew it was false through intuition. I thought it was religion. It appeared to be old stuff, not compared to my life as I 'ascended'. Here was I on the brink of 5D living, here to bring the light to humanity! But oh, how wrong I was! As the Bible says, "There is nothing new under the sun," and there certainly isn't.

The New Age repackages spiritual concepts to make it feel really forward-thinking, exciting, and cutting edge. But in reality, all of it has been said before; it's just the philosophy of Gnosticism repackaged. Gnosticism was exactly the heresy that Apostle Paul was addressing in his letters in the Bible, and he rebuked it. Gnosticism is basically the constant pursuit of hidden knowledge, or secret knowledge that we can only obtain with 'higher intelligence'. It's all within us, they say; we just have to know how to unlock it. Thousands of years later, we see the same story being packaged in different wrappers, and people are still searching for this secret knowledge. What kind of creator hides who they are? Not the kind of creator that is God, who wants relationship with His people.

False Belief Three: The Bible Has Been Manipulated

I'd openly admit one of the main things holding me back from becoming a Christian was that I was certain the Bible had been manipulated. I had always been told this and believed it, of course without ever researching or even reading the Bible myself. I remember at one point I thought God was sending me into the Christian faith because He needed me to decode the Bible in some way – that's the kind of ego I'd built up! Imagine, people have studied the Bible for thousands of years and God needed me to go in and decode it! Needless to say, this was a downright deception. But that was the plan: to read it and be able to identify what was truth and what was false; better yet, I could research where it got corrupted and then perhaps work things out from there.

Except when I researched the validity of scripture, it came up without any substantial errors. I was amazed at how much evidence there is to support the Bible being accurate – shocked in fact. It is so astounding to me how many myths about the Bible surface when you have the truth to compare it to. My preconceived idea was that the Bible was handed down from one translator to another, before it got into our hands. But what I found is that is not how the Bible was translated. The theory goes that the King James version was really corrupted it. The most recent translation of the bible such as the English Standard Version was copied from a full copy of the New Testament (the Codex Sinaiticus) from the 4th century, so we have copies to compare from eleven centuries before King James, and they do not contradict the King James Version. This proves the Bible wasn't corrupted by King James, as the manuscript we now have from centuries before shows that.

With regards to the Old Testament, there was the discovery of the Dead Sea scrolls in the 1940s. These were copies of the Old Testament on more than 800 documents made of animal skin, papyrus and even forged copper dating 1,000 years or older than any copies we already had. They were found to be 96% accurate in terms of the Bible we read today! Incredible! Evidence that God preserves His word!

There are variations found in scripture, of course, due to the different sources from which the translations were made. However nothing of fundamental importance to the Christian faith is challenged. So a classic variant may be, instead of Jesus Christ, they may have put Christ Jesus. This is so amazing; the Bible holds true today as it did back then, not to mention the number of manuscripts connected to Jesus. This amazed me but first allow me to provide some historical context. So, Julius Caesar we know a lot about, a historical figure who has been studied in many classrooms for years. Well, guess how many manuscripts we have connected to Caesar? Sixteen. That's it: just sixteen manuscripts connected to the life of Caesar, all that knowledge we have and sixteen manuscripts. By comparison we have 25,000 manuscripts connected to Jesus. Yes, that's the number. So rest assured I think we can safely say that Jesus lived as a figure in history and not only that but the evidence we have of His life and death is credible and reliable.

Again, we may ask ourselves how were the copies made? The scribes would copy each manuscript by hand. Now we have to make allowance for human error, which explains the variants. But one thing is definite: it would have been impossible to manipulate the Bible. Impossible! Because to do this you would have to call back every manuscript, then amend them one by one according to your choosing, and then reissue them. With thousands of manuscripts spreading all over the world we can say it was an impossible feat to locate every single manuscript in the first instance. In fact, as times goes on, we are discovering more and more manuscripts, and the more we discover, the more the credibility and validity of scripture that is so highly respected as a historical document in the scholarly world.

If the central truth of the Bible is the Resurrection, there were over 500 eyewitnesses of Jesus' resurrection. (see 1 Corinthians 15:5-7). What is even more amazing is the Bible had forty different authors writing over 1500 years on three different continents and, in spite of these different backgrounds, there is such consistency among them all and no contradictions. Prophecies about Jesus were given 700 years before Jesus' birth and He has fulfilled 80 percent of them, apart from the end time prophecies which have yet to be fulfilled. The fulfilled prophecies include things He couldn't have controlled such as where He would be born, that He would be crucified (even though crucifixion was a form of execution introduced by the Romans hundreds of years later), and where He would be crucified. Statisticians would tell you that the probability of fulfilling just eight prophecies is a trillion to one. Well, He fulfilled over three hundred!

Lastly, Jesus referred to the Old Testament consistently throughout His ministry, quoting from Deuteronomy, Exodus, Genesis, Daniel, Isaiah and the Psalms, to name a few. Jesus not only knew the scriptures, but He was also consistent is His use of scripture, and many of the Old Testament scriptures He cited in reference to Himself, He has already fulfilled. In the book of Luke, Chapter

24, the Road to Emmaus, the risen Christ tells the disciples how the scriptures point to Him.

Jesus was made God at the Council of Nicaea

This then brings me on to one of the biggest rumours in regard to scripture: that Jesus was made to be God in the Bible at the Council of Nicea! For those who are not aware, this was the first council in the Christian church, an event that was held in 325 AD with the intention of defining the Christian doctrine. This wasn't because there was confusion about the divinity of Christ because the Trinity, i.e., the concept of three persons in God, the Father, the Son and the Holy Spirit, was already being preached. Although the actual term 'Trinity' is not used in the Bible, the concept exists. Jesus does speak of such a Trinity when He tells the disciples, "Therefore go and make disciples of all nations, baptizing them in the name of the Father, and of the Son and of the Holy Spirit" (Matthew 28:19). Again in Genesis 1:1, it says "In the beginning God (*Elohim*) created the earth and the heavens" and in Genesis 1:26, God (*Elohim*) said, "Let us make man in **our** image, after **our** likeness ..." The Hebrew word for God, *Elohim,* which is plural, as well as the reference to "our" signifies more than one person in God. Later scriptures convincingly show that Jesus and the Holy Spirit were right there working with the Father.

The Council of Nicaea was held to **defend** the Trinity, not to create it. The reason for the meeting at the Council of Nicea was resolve Arianism (or the belief in one person as God) which was an attack on the Trinity and to denounce it as a heresy. (Apologist Wesley Huff does some serious work on early church history and, on this topic, specifically.)

So scripture upholds the Trinity. It shows Jesus, the Father and the Holy Spirit to be separate Persons, yet of the same divinity. When Jesus at the start of His Ministry was baptised in the Jordan by John the Baptist, we see clearly the full Godhead present. Look what the scripture says, "When all the people were being baptised, Jesus was baptised too. And as he was praying, heaven was opened and the Holy Spirit descended on him in bodily form like a dove. And a voice came from heaven: 'You are my Son, whom I love; with you I am well pleased'" (Luke 3:21-22). So here we have the Son come down to earth as man, the Holy Spirit overshadowing the event and the Father endorsing His Son.

False Belief Four: Women Are Suppressed in the Bible

Another myth I really believed was that all women are suppressed in the Bible and branded as prostitutes. I could write an entire book around the female empowerment movement and the manipulation of it. The Divine Feminine Goddess movement in the New Age is a massive part of the world stage propaganda just playing out for all to see. I was in deep with the Divine Goddess work; it was a big part of my life and work with my clients. One of my programs was named 'Divine Fem' and the major energy I called in to client sessions was Kuan Yin, Isis, Mother Mary, Mary Magdalene, and the like. I had worked with these so-called goddesses throughout my New Age participation, normally one for a month or so and then another would come into my life, especially Isis in the Mystery Schools.

In regard to the role of women in the Bible, we have to take into account the cultural context where women were seen in a very traditional role in society and were generally subservient to men. Even so, what I realised upon studying in the Bible is that God actually lifts women up both in the Old and New Testament. This is the complete opposite to what is spread around New Age circles. For example, in those days a woman's testimony wouldn't have been taken seriously. If a woman testified to something it wouldn't have been considered valid because their account would not be considered reliable.

So, what did God do? Well, it is interesting that the first person to whom Jesus appeared at His resurrection was Mary Magdalene (a once demonized woman who became a follower of Jesus). She was the first witness who went back and told the disciples. There are also books in the Bible about women (and minorities), for example, the book of Ruth where a Moabite woman named Ruth displays amazing courage and loyalty to her mother-in-law Naomi and embraces Naomi's God and her people. Ruth becomes the ancestor of Jesus. Then there is Esther, who became queen in Persia and through her bravery saved the Jewish people from annihilation. Don't forget Deborah, a Judge and prophetic woman who led the Israelites in battle against a formidable force, the Canaanites. God even pays tribute to a prostitute Rahab, who protected the two spies sent to Jericho before the taking of Jericho; she became part of the genealogy of Jesus as well.

No, women may have been suppressed by the culture but God through the prophets and Jesus Himself rescued them, elevated them, honoured them and recognised their contribution. When I read the Bible, I don't see any narrative of suppression of women; rather, I see God's grace and love for women.

False Belief Five: Any Type of Division is Bad

The New Age always taught me to steer clear of anything that caused division in any way, argh! What a perfect way to get people to instantly reject absolute truth because, of course, the truth rightly divides the truth from the lie. I can totally see this now as part of the wider agenda, the One World New Order that is being entrenched in government, religion and the economy (see Revelation 13 and 17 for more details). Christ not only spoke about division, *He came to bring division*! Luke 12:51: "Do you think that I came to give peace on earth? I tell you, not at all but rather division". He told us about the broad path to the evil one and the narrow path to His kingdom that only few find. The way of the cross (repentance and following Christ) is the opposite of this concept of 'oneness' where all are guaranteed salvation in a world where there is no sin. In fact, Christ preached about Hell more than He preached about Heaven; He preached division, the opposite of oneness. His concept of oneness is unity in Him (see John 17), while the idea of unity in the world system is a dangerous and misleading path to fall into. Jesus warned: "For wide is the gate and **broad is the road that leads to destruction, and many enter through it**. But small is the gate and narrow the road that leads to life, and only a few find it" (Matthew 7:13-14). As Adrian Rogers once said, "It is better to be divided in truth than united in error," and I couldn't agree more.

False Belief Six: The universe is God

This one astounded me. I never really noticed but I never really used to think of a God; it was more of a source, the original source of where everything came from. It was like an energy that flows through all things and in me too, which then makes me the creator. I used to say things like "the universe supports me"; but this seems so odd to me now. But it was like I was this divine being, connected to the universe and I could channel this energy to create. I've discovered that the belief in the universe being god is Pantheism, where everything is wrapped in the divine, including Gaia, mother earth. I'm so thankful that I now I have a relationship with a personal God, not some universal energy. He is my heavenly Father who walks with me through all the storms and victories in life. Nothing compares.

False Belief Seven: The World Is Determined by My Truth

I believed that truth was relative and not absolute. Whatever any-one believed was true, in the sense that it was their truth and therefore true for them, though maybe not true for me. Now I can see this doesn't even make sense. I used to completely reject the fact that absolute truth exists. Let's take this cup that I'm drinking out of whilst I type this ... beautifully made by a potter in Suffolk I managed to pick up in a charity store for a bargain of £2.50; it's brown with a lovely floral design on the front. Now that is either true or it isn't by fact. If someone comes along and calls it pink, just because they genuinely believe it's pink, that doesn't make it pink, by fact. Of course, they would be entitled to say it's pink and even believe it's pink, *but that doesn't make it true*. The belief the cup is both brown and pink can't be true either; it's either one or the other.

Similarly, a crime is committed and two witnesses are called to give an account of what they saw. The two accounts, if told truth-fully, will have essential similarities, though there may be some differences in the telling of it. One may have had a blind spot and couldn't actually have a clear view of the scene. The other may have had a large vehicle go past, which distorted their hearing. This means that the witnesses' focus may have been on different things, so either may have missed an important part of the event. Now, if both accounts contradict one another in critical areas, neither would be considered true. Both would be considered attempts to decipher what the truth actually was. But the court wishes to discover the absolute truth, not someone's perception of it. There can be a version of truth in each of the witnesses' minds, but then there is the objective truth of what actually happened.

Absolute truth is permanent and it cannot be exceeded or erased. It is true and will never change regardless of circumstances, feelings or perceptions. By its very nature it's unkillable.

Can you now see how the New Age has taken the word 'opinion' and then exchanged it for the word 'truth'? This again is all part of the conditioning for what's to come. I've experienced the effect this has had on my life and those in a similar state, and find that it only leads to chaos. We hear things, and if we don't like them, we can choose to reject them from our reality. In this way, we become ignorant and out of touch with what's really occurring, believing we can just build our own reality based on how we want things to be, ***not how they truly are***. This is such a great strategy of Satan's for encouraging ignorance to the gospel, as the sinner's message is always hard to hear for new believers. Many would not like it to be a part of their truth and therefore reject this as part of their ideal reality. This is largely relativism, based on the right to carve one's reality from one's perceptions. Sadly, a made-up world of our own ideals leads us further away from truth.

False Belief Eight: All Paths Lead to God / We Are All God

Many in the New Age also believe all paths lead to God. Now let's look at this from a wider lens. How can all roads lead to God, when factually they all contradict one another? Islam, Christianity, Hinduism, Buddhism, Taoism they **all** can't possibly be true. On broad moral principles they might, but if we were to look at the truth of what Jesus and the Bible say, we know there is a higher truth. Jesus said, "I am *the* way, *the* truth and *the* life; no comes to the Father except through me" (John 14:6). It is interesting how many religions do give praise to Jesus for being a prophet, an ascended master and the like. But Jesus only points people to the Father, Son and Holy Spirit as God. If Christianity is true, that means that the Fall took place. That means Satan would have to exist, which means that he would continue his work of deception, just as he deceived Eve. This is how we have false religions. I mean if we think about it, it does work.

Many people reject the Christian faith because they can't possibly comprehend the idea of one religion being true when there are so many, as did I for quite some time. I like Keith Green's view on this: every religion holds Jesus in high esteem, Buddhism, Islam, Hinduism, New Age; they all claim Jesus to be a highly enlightened being. But Jesus said, "I and the Father are one" (John 10:30). Doesn't that make Jesus God?

One of the heavy teachings in the New Age is we are God. We are the powerful ones and to believe in anything outside of yourself is to give your power away ... it's all about us, nothing else. How can we truly hold on to the view that believing in God is giving our power away, when He is the only reason we have that power, and life for that matter in the first place? You can't give your power away to the very source of where life itself came from. If there is a painting, there must be a painter. If there is a creation, there must be a creator.

So, there you have it. The Holy Spirit showed up and was guiding me to truth. Just to round this off, if what I've said hasn't convinced you that the Bible is worth considering, let me share something from experience: the Bible is profound. I have entered into a deep relationship with God through His word – it's incredible. Of course, we can speak to God without opening the Bible and talk to Him in prayer. But when we truly read the Bible, the words change you. They will sanctify you, and change your heart, your mind and spirit. He is splendid, glorious, caring, compassionate, convicting, merciful, justifying, mystifying, wholesome! And, lastly, God is love. It's all expressed through His word for you! Your Creator has written a love letter to you. Why not pick up the Bible and see what He has to tell you?

I think it would be good to add here, you can buy many bibles online for under £5, you know ... just saying.

And Jesus answered them, "See that no one leads you astray. For many will come in my name, saying, 'I am the Christ,' and they will lead many astray."

Matthew 24:4-5

False Christs vs. The Real Christ

One of the biggest pleasures, honours and gifts in my life other than my salvation alone is getting to know who Jesus truly is. He who gave me everlasting life, also teaches me how to walk in this one. Just being with Him is a gift. As mentioned in the previous chapter, there is so much talk about Jesus across the world and throughout history. Other religions as well refer to Him, and claim Him to be an amazing prophet or teacher. They may even promote Him. But, be warned: these are false Christs. It's not Christ as He claimed to be in the scriptures. There are many false Christs in the New Age deception and in this chapter, I will address three of the main ones.

Deception One: We Are All God

The book *A Course in Miracles* is heavily promoted by many false light teachers. This book claims to be a channelled message from a spirit that went by the name of 'Jesus'. This apparent spirit of Jesus wrote this book to share with humanity that the Bible and His teachings have long been misrepresented. As we know, Satan masquerades as an angel of light, so it makes sense he would portray himself as the ultimate light – Jesus. The book sounds very appealing to the ears – itching ears, one might say. However, once you compare this to scripture so many flaws are revealed. I also question how this message was given. Like many other new age channelled books, this can be a common theme among new age channelling writers; they can be reluctant to participate but the spirits persist relentlessly, until they give in.

The most popular claim from *A Course in Miracles* is the 'We Are All God' doctrine. This incorporates the belief that, when Jesus claimed to be the Son of God, He included in it the rest of us, meaning you and me. So the divinity He claimed is ours as well. We are all sons of God, and in a general sense this is true for believers: we are sons by adoption (Romans 8:16-18). This what the verses say: "For his Holy Spirit speaks to us deep in our hearts and tells us that we really are God's children. And since we are his children, we will share his treasures—for all God gives to his Son Jesus is now ours too. But if we are to share his glory, **we must also share his suffering**." Notice the proviso that we must share in His suffering. And indeed the whole context of Romans 8 is of those who are adopted into the family of God through their acceptance of Jesus Christ as Lord and Saviour. By making Him Lord over our lives, we become His followers or disciples.

However, the New Age has twisted this concept of sonship, by saying that Jesus wasn't claiming to be anything superior to the rest of us. He just understood His power was of a higher capacity than the rest of us. So we are all sons of God, just like Jesus, only He was aware of His divinity; we are not. *A Course in Miracles* says, "Is he the Christ? O yes, along with you". But there is a huge distinction between Jesus and us. We are not divine: we are created beings and we have all sinned. Only Jesus was of the Godhead and came to earth as a sinless being!

In contrast with the other Christs, when asked whether He was the Son of God, Jesus answered "Truly, truly, I say to you, before Abraham was, *I am*" (John 8:59). Now this is not the 'I AM' presence that the New Age has distorted it into. "I AM" here refers to God's name in the Bible. In the Book of Exodus in the Old Testament when Moses asked God His name, God replied, "I AM"; in Hebrew this is *Yahweh* or "I am the One who is". Hence when Jesus was asked this by the Jews, He used the same attribute! In other words, He was claiming to be God.

God has many names in the Bible because He has many characteristics. The name "I AM" represents who He is by nature – the "Self-existent One". God is the great "I AM" because He created the heavens and the earth; He was there in the beginning; He relies on nothing and is the ultimate power. We are not "I AM" – we exist because God created us, we live because God created food, we exist because our parents had sexual relations. We all are dependent on God: WE ARE BECAUSE HE IS. How could we ever conceive of putting ourselves in the same category as "I AM"? Jesus knew this. He was actually claiming to be God and even though He was born into this world as flesh, He was born of a virgin through the 'overshadowing' of the Holy Spirit. That is only possible for "I AM".

Jesus was crucified for claiming to be the Son of God. If Jesus did mean that He was just like the rest of us, then why did He allow Himself to be beaten, ridiculed and crucified for it? Why didn't He at least try to explain in what sense He was divine? After all, the concept of us all being gods isn't really that hard to explain. Then there's also the period of three years that He spent teaching His disciples – and indeed, the New Age regards Him as one of the highest vibrational spiritual teachers and prophets to have ever lived. If so, then why was He so inept at teaching His disciples about His own identity? Why were they all convinced He was God? Why did Apostle Peter describe Jesus as "Our God and Savior" (2 Peter 1:1)? Why, after He had trained them and given them instruction, did they preach the gospel: that Jesus died for their sins, was buried, and rose again three days later? How could they all have gone into such error having been trained by such a great teacher?

When we spend so much intensive time with a teacher (with in-struction and hands-on experience), it's very unlikely that any of us would come away with the opposite teaching to what has been imparted. So why, after being taught by Jesus for three years, did His disciples get things so distorted? It just doesn't make sense, especially as Jesus chose them to be His successors. He says in the book of John that He picked them because they were teachable, mouldable and in need of a saviour. He taught them well because they understood He was God, who died for the sins of the world, and they were able to spread the word of the gospel which was always the plan. If He told them to go out and spread the good news, would a high calibre teacher not check that they had the right information? The answer is clear, because the disciples got it right: Jesus is God.

But what really convinced me was a study of how Jesus referred to His Father. Do you know Jesus says "MY Father" in the gospels in over forty verses, and "OUR Father" only once? In the countless times He preached and spoke about the Father with the disciples, He always called God "MY Father". Yet when the disciples asked how to pray, Jesus did something interesting. He told them to say "Our Father" – this to me is mind blowing!! That's no way a coincidence. Jesus could state "My Father" because He is the Father's ONLY begotten Son. Yes, once we receive Christ, we become a child of God. Even so, Jesus was making a distinction between Himself and His disciples. I found that truly revealing. In the Jewish tradition the lineage would always come from the Father. Jesus was born of a virgin conceived by the Holy Spirit and therefore His direct descent would be our Heavenly Father, not an earthly father.

Still think we have the same divinity as Jesus? Praise God, He works in such beautiful and mighty ways. Do not believe all the myths.

Read the word of God for yourself and ask the Holy Spirit to guide you.

Deception Two: Christ Consciousness

Closely allied with the 'We Are All God' concept is 'Christ Consciousness'. This plays a massive part in the Starseed narrative and is by far the most popular and fast-growing new age teaching. What is it and what does it mean?

Christ consciousness is the belief that we are all Christ. It's a state ascending to the level of consciousness of Jesus Christ. New Age doesn't deny the miracles and healings performed by Christ. On the contrary, they see Him as a very high vibrational Master, essentially, someone that attained spiritual mastery in their lifetime. So Christ consciousness is the belief we all have this level of divinity available to us; therefore by growth and working on ourselves, we are all able to ascend to the same level of consciousness.

Therefore, many New Agers will enter a discussion about Christ consciousness with "We are Christ", or "I am Christ as you are too", believing we all have the potential to operate on the same level of consciousness as Christ. The claim it's up to us to just tap into this spiritual realm to unlock it. They interpret this belief by saying that Christ was just someone that managed to attain a certain level of wisdom and knowledge. "He is God – but so are you and I – and we all can attain this and awaken this consciousness within us. Jesus just managed to attain that level of enlightenment." As you can see, as with the author of *A Course in Miracles*, they are strongly influenced by both eastern mysticism and gnosticism, which propound the theory that secret wisdom can only be obtained by the enlightened ones. Interestingly, there is never any mention of sin.

It's strange, looking at it now, how the New Age seems to perpetuate the feeling of lack. In their philosophy, something always needs to be unlocked; some hidden knowledge needs to be found. It's a constant quest to be fulfilled. On the other hand, the Bible says we are complete in Christ, "And because you belong to Christ you are complete, having everything you need. Christ is ruler over every other power and authority" (Colossians 2:10 ERV).

I really like how Steve Bancarz breaks this down in his YouTube video *Christ Consciousness Debunked by Jesus*. I have condensed his words to give an overview. Steve takes us to Matthew 24, where Jesus is warning His disciples about the coming deception that will arise before His second coming, and the signs of the end times.

"Take heed that no one deceives you. For many will come in My name, saying, 'I am the Christ,' and will deceive many" (Matthew 24:4-5). Now we might be led to think this would mean people claiming to be Jesus; however, this isn't the case as few claimed to actually be Jesus. When Jesus says "many will come in my name," the "many" would refer to a high volume of the population. I believe here He is referring to claims such as Christ Consciousness perpetuated in *A Course in Miracles* and many new age writings that will deceive many. In other words, Jesus Himself is warning people to steer away from philosophies like Christ Consciousness by telling us many people will say, "I am Christ" and be deceived.

One thought that always shows up so clearly to me is that I have never met anyone that taught Christ Consciousness and at the same time healed and performed miracles like Christ. Many have claimed to have activated their 'Christ Consciousness', but with no evidence to show or fruits to actually reveal this.

However, Christians do have Christ living inside of them, dwelling in our hearts. But this is gained through receiving Christ through God's grace, through His gift of salvation, not through any striving to reach 'Christ Consciousness' by any means outside the Bible.

Deception Three: Jesus Was a Starseed

Lastly, and likely the most relevant to this book, there are claims Jesus was a Starseed. This theory has no evidence or proof to back it up whatsoever; it is simply just a theory that's been generated from the Starseed narrative. In the Bible, Jesus claims to be sent from heaven: "**I have come down from heaven,** not to do my own will but the will of him who sent me" (John 6:38). There is nothing in scripture to suggest that Jesus claimed to be a Starseed; however, there is ample evidence that He claimed to be God.

One of the main objectives of Satan is to keep us away from God's word. It's amazing to me how many people claim to know things about Jesus but have never read the Bible, which is, in fact, the closest account we have of His life. Due to that, my perception of Christian teaching prior to reading the Bible was totally distorted. I thought that God looked down on humanity and saw they were in trouble and so He morphed into a man and came down to earth. It was for this reason that Jesus was created. But let's take a look at the supremacy of Christ according to the book of Colossians, another book that opened my mind.

"He is the image of the invisible God, the firstborn of all creation. For by him all things were created, in heaven and on earth, visible and invisible, whether thrones or dominions or rulers or authorities—all things were created through him and for him. And he is before all things, and in him all things hold together" (Colossians 1:15-17). This blew my mind when I read it: Jesus was always there from the beginning. Everything was made through Him and for Him. Jesus was not sent from another Starseed System to help humanity. Humanity was created through Him! ALL THINGS were made through Him. Just think about that, everything was made through Jesus – that's all-living things, every blade of grass and drop of water, every living being, including you and me! Jesus is God because He was there even before the earth was made.

Jesus made claims that could only be made if He was God. In Matthew 11:28, He promises all who are weary and burdened to come to Him and He will give them rest for their souls. Jesus is directing people to Himself as the one that can give them rest for their souls. In addition, in Matthew 28:18, He declares that all authority *in heaven* and earth has been given to Him. Jesus is claiming to be equal with God, which is why the Pharisees found it to be blasphemy.

Not only that, **we were made for Him, for Jesus**, for a relationship with Him. It all began with Him, and it will all end with Him. The book of Revelation talks about the end times, where it refers to Jesus' return: "I am the Alpha and the Omega, the first and the last, beginning and the end." So to call Jesus a Starseed is outright heresy. But most of all, it is an insult to His true nature and divinity. He is so much greater! He is what is holding all things together! Christ is everything! In the new age I was always researching ancient knowledge, ancient secrets and the like. Well, Jesus Christ is the ultimate ancient path, the way, the only rest for your soul. Apostle Paul expressed that all wisdom and knowledge are hidden in Christ: "In him lie hidden all the treasures of wisdom and knowledge" (Colossians 2:3).

The New Age portrays Jesus as just another stepping stone on the path, when in reality He is the entire path, He is every stepping-stone, the river, land, and ocean, and more. Jesus is "THE way, THE truth and THE life". He is the "door" to salvation; He is the "light of the world" (John 14:6; 10:9: 8:12). He was there from the beginning: "In the beginning was the Word, and the Word was with God, and the **Word was God**. He was with God in the beginning. Through him all things were made; without him nothing was made that has been made. In him was life, and that life was the light of all mankind. The light shines in the darkness, and the darkness has not overcome it" (John 1:1-5).

Let's back up for a moment: "In the beginning was the word" – we know the "word" to be Jesus. The "word was with God and the word was God" – so Jesus was with God and He was God; He is part of the Trinity. Through Him all things were made. In Him was life and this was the light of ALL mankind!! Jesus had always been there, and ALL things were created through Him. Jesus IS God and the darkness could not overcome Him. As man, He overcame the darkness that day at Calvary. That day the light won – Jesus won. That's why Jesus' last words were, "It is finished!" because He accomplished His mission – He overcame sin and death. In John 16:33 Jesus said, "In the world you will have tribulation; but be of good cheer, I have overcome the world" – and He did, through the finished work of the cross. The poetry in my heart is just captivated by the book of John: everything in my being knows that Jesus is truth when I read these words. Thank God for the Holy Spirit revealing this to us!

"The true light that gives light to everyone was coming into the world. He was in the world, and though the world was made through him, the world did not recognise him. He came to that which was his own, but his own did not receive him. Yet to all who did receive him, to those who believed in his name, he gave the right to become children of God—children born not of natural descent, nor of human decision or a husband's will, but born of God" (John 1:9-13).

This verse breaks my heart. Can you imagine people so caught up in their worldly ways with their pride and sin that their God and

Saviour is standing right before them, and they reject Him? They do not recognise Him; they do not and will not receive Him. This makes my heart bleed. This is as true today as it was 2,000 years ago that people reject Jesus, and they will not receive Him and His gift of salvation. I was once was one of them. But for those who choose to believe, we enter God's adopted family to be reborn of God through the gift of salvation, and come into a relationship with our heavenly Father as children of God. Salvation is to be saved from the destructive power of sin, and to go from spiritual death to *eternal life* and newness of life here and now.

"**The Word became flesh** and made his dwelling among us. We have seen his glory, the glory of the one and only Son, who came from the Father, full of grace and truth" (John 1:14). Jesus became a man in the flesh: the **word of God, God Himself** 2,000 years ago **walked this earth among us**.

I hope you can see the true beauty and wonder that is Jesus Christ, the Son of God. In the beginning was the Word, the Word was with God and the word **was** God ... and the word became flesh and dwelt among us.

Jesus was and is the word of God and, as the Bible says, He is the same "yesterday, today and forever" (Hebrews 13:8).

"When you are in distress and all these things have come upon you, in the latter days you will return to the Lord your God and listen to His voice."

Deuteronomy 4:30

Father, You've Always Been There

Some Christians have a distinct moment when they felt born again, or a memorable experience that accompanies this. However, God works differently in each of us whilst always remaining faithful to scripture. I can't remember the exact moment that I really believed. But I can remember one pivotal moment leading up to it. It was a very surreal moment and as if it were all happening in slow motion.

It was like there was a movie reel of my life playing out before me slide by slide. I was seeing selected events from the past in a completely different light. The first slide was a memory of when I was just a little girl. I never even remember believing in Jesus back then. I remember I was in my room just before bed. The next day was one of the biggest days of my life as an eight-year-old; it was the school district sports. This race was especially important as my friend Gemma who I had beaten all last season, was winning races this season. I came second to her on the previous meet. I had been training hard with my dad and I didn't want to let us down. I remember just praying to God to help me win the race. I truly believed God was there and that He would be with me the next day. He was! I won that race, all glory to Him! But it wasn't the win that God was recalling: it was my faith in that prayer, in Him.

The second memory was in my classroom aged sixteen. In the UK at fifteen we had to choose certain classes; the options we had to pick from were from groups of three. I remember in one particular category I disliked all three options, Cookery, Information Technology, or Religious Education. Mum said she would teach me to cook, I couldn't stand IT, so RE seemed the best of a bad bunch. To my surprise I loved it. I remember being extremely interested in Christianity, even though I was 'off the rails' at this point. Due to all the changes in my personal life, I performed well below my potential in all my exams. I even bunked (skipped) my PE and got caught ... but for Religious Education I got an A. This particular memory was of Mrs. Orit, my schoolteacher, who had the word 'ATONEMENT' written on the board, but she had broken it down to 'AT-ONE with God'. This stayed with me forever. Jesus atoned for our sins so we could become at-one-with the Father. It was so amazing to me that God was working in my life all this time. Who would have thought years later that one lesson helped lead me to Christ. To think God was weaving in my life back then!

The third slide was a memory of when I decided to do a water fast. I fasted often in the New Age due to its physical healing and spiritual benefits as I found it helped draw out suppressed emotion. It was the fourth day with no food, just water. Then something very beautiful happened. I get to the afternoon, and I have the place to myself and I'm starting to feel uncomfortable. Now at this point, I'm a pro at 'releasing', so I grab my yoga mat, place it in the beaming sunshine on the balcony and I sit down cross-legged with my palms up in the air saying the words, "I'm ready to feel you now, whatever this is; I welcome you and I'm ready to feel". I used to welcome such healing because I felt it was all the stuff I had to clear as a Starseed to do my part for humanity.

Then it came ... the memory of a time I got very drunk and acted inappropriately. Tears begin to roll down my face. I embraced that flash point like I always did in my healing sessions as I knew releasing this was for my highest good and containing it would only hold me back. But this healing session was taking a different turn. I was starting to feel a level of guilt and shame I'd never felt before. Instead of releasing emotion because I felt like I had been wrongly carrying shame, I felt like I had 'dishonoured something', and that 'something' *wasn't about me.*

I couldn't really make sense of what was happening. My crying was getting louder than usual. Mindful the neighbours may hear, I ran from the balcony into the house. As soon as I entered the living room, I fell to my knees and cried out to God, "I'm so sorry" over and over again. I couldn't really fully understand what was happening. All I know is what my body and spirit longed to do – naturally. I didn't have Jesus in mind, or sin for that matter. I hadn't even come across Christianity since school. But I felt a deep regret and sorrow for the thing I had previously done, and it's shocking to me that my natural instinct after a four-day fast was to fall to my knees before God. It still amazes me now. I didn't know I was repenting; it just came so naturally.

What does that say about what's really going on with us? Even after this experience, I still didn't fully understand it. I even made a YouTube video about my fast and referred to day 4 as 'clearing guilt and shame'. However, I certainly didn't mention I dropped to my knees. Months later I'm having this experience with God and He is showing me all the time He was there, working in me and around me. I was in awe. So getting on my knees wasn't something I viewed as fearful or powerless after this reminder; in my fasting state, that's what I chose to do of my own accord. I was spontaneously coming to God in remorse, not by someone telling me I needed to do it, but by wanting to.

It's strange to think that at the time how I believed repentance was giving our power away. To get on your knees before a holy God and apologise is therefore a weakness. At the time I believed 'we' are God' 'we' are the power. But it seems after that fast I could see more clearly and differently. What I couldn't see at the time is how this very belief that I am God had bred pride, and how we could believe that bowing to our Creator is beneath our dignity. I was truly so far gone, and I couldn't even sense it in the slightest.

The fourth memory was when I bought a book on the *Galactic Federation*. This is supposedly a galactic counsel that governs the universe. Of course, they claim to hold wisdom and knowledge that we don't know here on earth. Their channelled messages normally consist of how the earth is in trouble and the messages we receive from the council will save the planet. I was still living as a Starseed and had listened to some of the leading channellers and was 'feeling a pull' towards the Galactic Federation. I remember speaking to Mark, who was still a mentor, although I was doing much on my own now. All he said was, "Just ask to be protected from any programming before you read it," as he was unsure. He had never had any experience with the Galactic Federation but he had heard there were two, the Galactic Federation and the Galactic Federation of Light. One was supposedly dark but he couldn't remember which one. At the time I thought Mark was being paranoid, but I asked for protection nonetheless.

As I started to read the book, the second or third chapter said that if you come and work for the Galactic Federation, you will never go without anything. The way it was worded, was not in the sense of "We will provide", but more along the lines of "We will give you the lifestyle if you join us". I remember the text was very manipulative and it instantly raised red flags, so much so that I decided not to carry on reading as it felt like some kind of deal.

Anyhow, days later Mark picked me up for the 'energy' work we used to do with the land. On this specific day we were headed for a long drive. But I started to feel really ill and dizzy, and told Mark.

He started to ask me questions about what I had done recently. About thirty minutes later, the feeling became too intense and I cried out, "Stop the car I need to get out!" Mark pulled over immediately and guess where we were? Right outside a church. We swiftly walked in the church grounds, and I started to feel worse. When I used to release, I always burped and, in extreme cases, was sick – but that was very rare. It seemed normal as energy was being released out of my body; it needed a means to escape, so my body seemed to burp it out. I remember breaking dark vows once, and that came back to me, so I just started declaring and affirming that all ties with evil were broken. Then I really started to burp violently, more like gagging and coming right from my stomach. I was cutting all ties through all dimensions of space and time and so I thought I was just releasing myself from past lives.

But all I kept thinking about was that Galactic Federation book. So I started to degree and declare cutting all ties with that book and the Galactic Fed, Immediately, my body really started to react. I was gagging up 'energy' – I don't know how else to explain it – and then fluid kept coming up into my mouth, so I had to keep spitting. My eyes were watering, my face was completely red. This went on for about half an hour and I was exhausted. Fortunately, no one came into the church grounds.

As my memories were being played out, God showed me He had led to me to that church. It's as if he was showing me that church-yard was a sign of purification. I don't know the actual details of what happened in that churchyard, but what I know for sure is somehow God had a hand on that situation. I wasn't ready to meet Jesus that day; I was still in so deep in my deception. Now God has the power to convert anyone at any time, but what I do know is at that time, God had not worked on my heart as much as He has now. I was still so full of pride, and even now I'm certainly not completely free. But the contrast is like night and day. I thank God He worked in me the way He did, so I was able to hear and see the truth of the gospel. Praise You Father; praise You!

That experience made me realise God has always been there, even though I had abandoned Him. I have reflected on more areas of my life since then, and I realise He had been trying to get my attention. People think God is this judgemental Father who rules with an iron fist, but in reality, He is a Father that loves you and is trying to be in relationship with you, trying to get your attention without forcing your will. Can you notice Him trying to get your attention?

"For God so loved the world that he gave his one and only Son, that whoever believes in him shall not perish but have eternal life."

John 3:16

The Good News

From discovering that my guides were deceptive, it took me a few months to fully accept the gospel of Jesus Christ. How could I know I needed to be found by Christ when I was unaware I was lost? How could I truly be forgiven for my sins and experience the magnitude of His grace when I was not aware that I was a sinner? How could I truly know that there is a God who loves me so much He sacrificed His only Son so I could be saved, when I really didn't think I needed saving? How could I receive the gift of life that Jesus brings, when I had no idea, I was dead? All this took a while for my mind to open, and for the Holy Spirit to work in me.

This part of my journey, my conversion, was the best part. Now I'd reached the stage where I could see the false light clearly, I knew scripture is reliable, I could see the false Christ red flags and I was coming to know Jesus as He truly is. I was so scared to give my heart to the Lord; but as I was reading scripture and coming to know God's truth, that foreboding was being replaced by a yearning for Christ. It was the point where my heart, my logic, intellect and experience were all coming into agreement. All my questions had been answered and I now asked myself, *What does it all mean?*

It means when Jesus said the words "I am the way, the truth and the life and no one comes to the Father except through me"... that means I must understand that's what Jesus believed and preached. That means He didn't teach oneness for its own sake. The fact that Jesus spoke about hell more than heaven in the Bible shows He believed in hell. Jesus didn't make fun or joke about Satan. He affirmed him to be real and to be taken seriously. This also means that Jesus of Nazareth understood the sins of man and the sins of the world. It meant that one day on Calvary, over 2,000 years ago, even though He was in complete control of the situation, He allowed Himself to be mocked, beaten, ridiculed for *our* sake – me and you.

This also means that we were born into a sinful world as a result of the fall, and we all fall short of the glory of God. We are sinners and the wages for sin is death (separation from God). Because God is holy and just, the wages must be paid. But this is the incredible thing about Our Father. He sent His only begotten Son, Jesus Christ, to take that penalty *for* us, so we would not perish but have everlasting life. God revealed His plan for His victory over sin as early as Genesis, right from the fall. God sent people to prophecy about the coming Messiah – that He would die for our transgressions and by His wounds we would be healed hundreds of years before Jesus (see Isaiah 53:5). Later Jesus would do exactly that.

Our Saviour, Jesus of Nazareth, was tortured, whipped, in agony and bleeding, and carried His cross to His own place of execution, where He allowed the sins of the world to be cast upon Himself. He did all this so you and I could walk free from the power of our sin.

It just really hit home. ***Christ was crucified for my sake. For all our sakes.***

This all happened! This really happened!

Not only that, but He was also buried; then three days later He rose from the dead, so we could be justified. He came back to life and prepared His disciples to spread the message of the gospel, and then He ascended to heaven where He sits at the right hand of the Father. This is what He brings – **Jesus brings life** – He came back to life and when we receive Him, we receive life, too! We are born again through Christ; without being born again we cannot see the Kingdom of God. Jesus preached "Truly, truly, I say to you, unless one is born of water and the Spirit, he cannot enter the kingdom of God. That which is born of the flesh is flesh, and that which is born of the Spirit is spirit. Do not marvel that I said to you, 'You must be born again'" (John 3: 5-7). Jesus is Lord and Saviour; He saves us from our sin and washes us anew.

What a joy and blessing! Being born again changed my life in so many ways. But one of the most powerful is a thirst for that which is real. My desires and wants before seemed so shallow. I have come to desire the richness of the life that He offers. This isn't material, or circumstantial, nothing we can measure by worldly standards. It's the inner flow of living water inside of us from knowing who He is and living on His word. It makes me feel alive. The more I know Him, the more I yearn to know Him more because He is the only thing that can satisfy my soul.

Life in this sinful world is temporary, but life in restored relationship to the Father is eternal. In order for us to go to heaven where God dwells, we must accept Jesus. God doesn't force us to love Him; He has given us a choice between our sinful life and Jesus. If we choose to reject the gift of salvation, then the word of God says we are destined for hell. I know this may be a hard concept for many to take in, as the new age does such a good job of ridiculing the notion of hell and eternal punishment. But please, just think about the consequences if what the Bible and Jesus teaches is true. I beg you, please don't judge the message on whether it feels good, but whether what you are hearing is the truth.

Jesus was the only sinless being to ever walk the earth, He not only died for us, but He also lived a righteous life for us so He could transfer His righteousness to us. "For God made Christ, who never sinned, to be the offering for our sin, so that we could be made right with God through Christ" (2 Corinthians 5:21). Not only that, but this gift is free. We don't have to do anything for this except believe in Him and His work on the cross. There is no 'next level'; there no activation, no code or hidden knowledge to unlock. **Come just as you are ... He came for sinners.** Jesus died for you, for me and the sins of the world. But we can only receive this through grace when we accept this truth and believe in Him and what He did for us on the cross.

We are **all** sinners ... we have all fallen short of the glory of God. There is no one in history that is sinless other than Jesus. This is not giving your power away: it's standing on the truth. The consequences of the fall where Adam and Eve sinned against God were that we became sinful by nature. When this truth is accepted and acknowledged, it sets us free, reconnecting to the One that gave us any kind of power in the first place, our Creator! We are all trying to survive in a sinful world, surrounded by sin and living a life of sin, but it is sin that separates us from God. This world is hard, and God didn't create man to be trapped in sin, and He has provided the solution. He sent Jesus! He came for us.

"For God did not send his Son into the world to condemn the world, but in order that the world might be saved through him. Whoever believes in him is not condemned, but whoever does not believe is condemned already, because he has not believed in the name of the only Son of God" (John 3:17-18).

My hope is that you are not only reading these words, but truly hearing them. As I write this, my heart aches for people to understand this truth. Jesus died for you because He loves you. God loves you, and by the grace of God, we have this gift of salvation.

Jesus once said and continues to say, "**Come to me**, all you who are weary and burdened, and **I will give you rest**. Take my yoke upon you and learn from me, for I am gentle and humble in heart, and you will find rest for your souls. For my yoke is easy and my burden is light" (Matthew 11:28-30). Notice Jesus says, "**Come to me**", not the universe, not yourself. Go to Jesus! And He said **He will give you rest**! Hallelujah!

This isn't a phase thing, or a 'try this for a while thing'. Jesus died for us on the cross. He gives us new life, a new heart, a new mind, a new spirit, the Holy Spirit! My heart truly aches for those that have yet to find Christ. It's torture watching people deny what He has done for them; so many people are crying out for a Saviour but unable to see they need one, just like I was. There is a God who loves you, cares for you and His will is for you to believe in His Son. Jesus said, "For it is my Father's will that everyone who looks to the Son and believes in Him shall have eternal life". Jesus has given us God's will and it's to believe in Jesus. Why? Because that's how God can be in relationship with you! Through His Son, *God wants a relationship with you*.

It seems the various interpretations of Jesus are happy to accept everything Jesus did, but nothing that He said. But He said so much. When we read the Bible, Jesus' words are always pointing to the cross. It's amazing what He left the world with especially in the Sermon on the Mount in the book of Matthew. Just in the opening chapter He takes us through what real blessings are, and He opens our eyes to see our longing for a shallow and selfish existence. Sometimes I just think of what it must have been like to hear the greatest teaching ever heard. I sometimes imagine Jesus walking up the mountain in preparation, the sound of His worn sandals hitting the gravel path while He worked His way up, step by step. Was there anticipation in the air? Was there a sense in people that they were about to hear greatness? What was going through His mind whilst walking up that hill? I truly wonder what it must have been like to have been there to hear a message that would reverberate outwards to humanity until the end of time till He returns. I wonder if those there knew they'd heard the greatest sermon ever preached. I wonder if just being in His presence was overwhelmingly for those open to receive Him.

The very first words He shares in this powerful sermon are, "Blessed are the poor in spirit, for theirs is the kingdom of heaven." Those are the very first words from His lips in the entire sermon, a sermon where He shares how to enter the Kingdom, stay in the Kingdom, and follow Him. Why are these His first words? Because this is the first step for everyone. Unless we take this first step, that is, acknowledge we are poor and naked and sinful, we cannot enter the Kingdom of heaven. Sadly, many will never get this far. I pray the Lord softens their hearts.

"Blessed are the poor in spirit, for theirs is the Kingdom of heaven". At first glance, this doesn't even make sense, right!? How can the poor in spirit be blessed enough to enter the Kingdom of heaven? In the New Age everything is about raising our vibration, stepping into our power, owning our sovereignty, so this sounds very contradictory to anything we've been taught. How could this be? For this to fall into place, we must understand **the work of the cross**.

To be poor in spirit is to arrive at the reality that we need a saviour, that we are sinners, and we so desperately need Jesus. To be poor in spirit, we must accept that we are nothing without Jesus. It's not giving our power away because it's an illusion that we even have any without Him in the first place. This is why we are so blessed when we realise we are poor in spirit, because ours is the Kingdom of Heaven. Praise God!

I remember saying these words: "Dear Father, I know I'm a sinner, and I know You sent Your Son who died on the cross for my sins, and then You raised Him from the dead three days later. I accept Jesus as my Lord and Saviour. Please come into my life, in Jesus' name. Amen."

Being saved is the best thing that can happen to us, it's just simply amazing!! There is a reason why so many Christians get saved and then talk nonstop about Jesus and just desire to bring glory to His name. Because we are the born again. No paying for energy sessions, activations, attunements, or readings; just receive Him and His gift through grace. How beautiful that is! We don't have to work for His love; we don't have to try and raise our vibration to a certain frequency, or unlock some code: we just believe in Him and the cross. Truly, truly, we are so blessed!

This is just like Peter's mother in the gospel of Mark. She is sick in bed. Jesus comes in and lifts her out of bed and simply heals her by touch! She is completely healed, so what does she do next? She begins to serve them immediately. This is exactly what it's like when our lives are touched by Jesus. We instantly want to get up and serve others for His sake. That's the impact of what we experience, because the gift we have received is so precious that all we want is for people to know who He is and bring glory to His name.

Praise God, praise Him for all of it! I will praise Him for the rest of my days! His love is unsearchable and beyond anything I can put into words. Praise you Father, for it all!

Jesus saved me from my sin, saved me from demonic oppression, saved me from being trapped in these endless cycles of healing, saved me from trying to save myself but, most importantly, Christ saved my soul, and you know what? He has offered all this to you too.

All you need to be saved is **believe.**

"And no wonder, for Satan himself masquerades as
an angel of light."

2 Corinthians 11:14

Twisted Lies

S o, I did it. I put my faith in Jesus. I started to get into the Word
and go to church. I discovered worship. I removed occult
items from the house, and turned from my sin. The more I walked
the path of truth, the more I began to see how my previous new
age path was just a counterfeit of the real light. I've come to learn
that Satan cannot create anything; he counterfeits everything that
is genuine; he twists and manipulates the truth that leads us down
dark alleys. He is the ultimate deceiver.

You may be thinking, *But Sarah the new age stuff can work,* and I
would agree in the respect that it can lead to results. And that's
the whole point of false light, isn't it? It needs to look real and
feel real. Without any semblance of authenticity to the receiver, it
wouldn't be fake. When I grew up, we went through a phase of
wearing imitation bags, Louis Vuitton, Chanel – you name it –
I had one. I was in my twenties, walking around with a bag that
was supposedly meant to be anything from £500-£1k. On a school
leaver's salary! They were very good counterfeits; they looked like
the real deal. The majority of people I knew didn't know they were

fake. However, if someone walked in that had the real version, they would have been able to spot the fake immediately. Why? Because now they know the genuine bag – how the zip moves, how strong the buttons are and how the material feels. They'd know the authentic version so well it wouldn't take them long to recognise the fake. On the other hand, there were so many that had never even seen an authentic version, so for them, this looked like the real deal.

This is how it feels when we've found Jesus after living in the New Age. Because you have received the authentic version, the true love, the sacrificial love, the love of one laying down His life for you, you can see the rip off version for exactly what it is: the False Light that is the New Age.

Jesus warns us about false light in the Bible. The word "deceive" is in the New Testament over 35 times. It is frequently addressed for good reason. 2 Corinthians 11:14 says, "For even Satan disguises himself as an angel of light". This disguise is supposed to mimic the exact same experience and feel like the genuine article; it's supposed to appear to give off the same results. We are meant to feel like we have the real thing – that's the entire aim of a counterfeit.

That's why the New Age can parade as your Saviour. It's a counterfeit of the true salvation and life that we experience in Jesus Christ. I can most certainly admit there is so much that is appealing about the false light as it speaks to our flesh. It's no wonder so many are drawn to it, I would say I was romanced and seduced by the teachings. The book of Ecclesiastes states, "There is nothing new under the sun" and this is so true. We can trace this deception back to the Garden of Eden where Satan's lies seduced Eve. Adam and Eve lived in what we may consider as paradise, but when Adam and Eve sinned, known as the Fall, we then became spiritually dead.

Satan uses different tactics to deceive; some are out-and-out lies, but most of the time where it can appear convincing is when it's not all lies. The basis is truth but he bends the truth, sometimes ever so slightly in order to send someone in the wrong direction, away from God. How did Satan manage to convince Eve to sin against God? Let's take a look at the scripture to identify where Satan is still using the same devices amongst us today.

Let's look at **Genesis 3:**

The serpent (Satan) was the shrewdest of all the wild animals the Lord God had made. One day he asked the woman, "Did God really say you must not eat the fruit from any of the trees in the garden?"

"Of course we may eat fruit from the trees in the garden," the woman replied.

"It's only the fruit from the tree in the middle of the garden that we are not allowed to eat. God said, 'You must not eat it or even touch it; if you do, you will die.'"

"You won't die!" the serpent replied to the woman.

"God knows that your eyes will be opened as soon as you eat it, and you will be like God, knowing both good and evil."

The woman was convinced. She saw that the tree was beautiful, its fruit looked delicious, and she wanted the wisdom it would give her. So she took some of the fruit and ate it. Then she gave some to her husband, who was with her, and he ate it, too.

At that moment their eyes were opened, and they suddenly felt shame at their nakedness. So they sewed fig leaves together to cover themselves. (Genesis 3:1-6)

I'm sure you can already see so much in this scripture that reveals how Satan works. Let me share just four areas of deception:

Focus on Lack

Adam and Eve were living in abundance, not lacking anything. All this beauty, love, prosperity and security were available to them freely. What did Satan do? He focused their attention on their lack, what they couldn't do and have. They had so many trees available to them except for one tree, Satan took their eyes off all their blessings and onto that one tree they didn't have. A tactic that is commonly used by Satan – to take our attention off God's word and our current blessings and train it on our lack. This is why so many of us instantly reject Christianity: we instantly focus on the lack, the things we can't do.

The Bait of Wisdom and Power

Eve took a bite out of the forbidden fruit because she was led to believe she would receive higher wisdom. Satan encourages the same thought process in the new age because we love to possess hidden knowledge or secret wisdom. It's so attractive and seductive that our flesh will always want that power in one way or another – whether it's to reach enlightenment, be seen or admired, achieve something deemed successful, accumulate wealth, the list goes on. It's the promise of unlocking that secret wisdom and knowledge. In the New Age, with the promise of the 5D version of us, we chase the power. We forget that any power we possess is a gift, as is life from our Creator, and so we fall for the same old lie ... that we can be "like God".

Doubt about God

Satan made Eve doubt the intentions of God, implying that God's command to not eat from the tree was not in their best interests: He was holding back something from them. Again, this is so common. Satan will always plant these types of doubts in our mind: how can God love you if He hasn't given you a husband? How can God love us if war exists? How can God love us if there is suffering in the world? How can God love me if I've had such a hard life? All these things challenge our perception of God's love and intentions for us, so we have a distorted image of our heavenly Father.

Revelation of *Half* Truths

Satan convinced Eve they would be like God, knowing good and evil. This isn't an outright lie, but it's a half-truth. What Satan did here was to word the proposition in such a way that made attractive. He offered the power but didn't share the price they would pay: separation from God and the presence of evil in their lives. Satan will offer us truths that are scriptural and the new age derives many teachings from the Bible (positive thinking, self-care, self-reflection, consideration for others etc.). These bring blessings and progress in our lives, but we are receiving half-truths. The underlying message of the entire Bible, from beginning to end is the gospel of Jesus Christ. How can we receive such profound teaching from the Bible, yet not be aware of the true gift within the scriptures, our salvation? It's like receiving the shiny wrapper without the gift.

"You can be like God"

The deadliest of all – Satan wants us to believe we have the potential to be gods. That way we forget we even have a Maker, and we turn spirituality into self-worship rather than praise for God. Or, in some cases, we worship the creation, and not the creator. We make ourselves the most important piece of the puzzle, not realising the outcome is going to be catastrophic. Now, I don't want to get this distorted. Yes, we are here for amazing things as life is amazing and God created us in His image; but we are not the centrepiece of the universe. However, the context in which things are taught in the New Age, is that all attention is constantly on ourselves. Everything comes from within, "You are the universe" is a subtle way of focusing constantly on ourselves and leading us to believe that, by doing so, we are doing God's work.

Here are some of the ways the New Age counterfeits the Kingdom:

GOD'S GIFT	SATAN'S COUNTERFEIT
Being born again	Spiritual 're-birth' or awakening
Biblical tongues	Light language
Prophecy	Divination
Deliverance	Entity removal
Laying of hands	Reiki
Relationship with our Heavenly Father as His child	Re-parenting yourself
Understanding the fall of man	The Fall of Atlantis
Jesus is Saviour	Spiritual experiences coming as Saviour
Prayer	Affirmations
Blessings	Manifestation
Sanctification	Ascension
Yielding to God	Surrendering to the universe
The Holy Spirit	False spirits (i.e Kundalini spirit)
Miracles	Magic
Love	Flattery

The Genuine vs. the Counterfeit

For me, acknowledging that Satan is real and that he holds the levers in our world today was not an easy thing to accept. But now that I know that truth, I see it everywhere – in government and big business, in every school curriculum, in every media outlet, anything that goes by the name of entertainment.

Jesus referred to Satan as the enemy, the evil one, a liar, a murderer. But note that He also called him "the ruler of this world" (John 12:31; 14:30). That's because since the fall we came under the influence of Satan who has blinded our minds. It's only when we see the light of Jesus Christ and accept the gift of salvation that we can come back into relationship and be reconciled with God.

Satan may be "the ruler of this world" because of man's rebellion and choice to live in darkness, but the moment we see the light we can make Jesus our King.

"If we say that we have no sin, we deceive ourselves, and the truth is not in us."

1 John 1:8

I'm Sorry, Father, Please Forgive Me

It was not until I started to read the Bible, to get to know Jesus and who He is that I began to understand how defiled my life had been. Part of our salvation process is repentance, for sin is what has truly kept man separated from the Father. As we discussed earlier, the word 'sin' simply means to 'miss the mark' or 'miss the goal' to denote our failure to walk in obedience to God's word and commandments. In this, we are effectively choosing to live the way we want instead of how our Creator desires us to live and treat others. When we truly believe, we then realise how we have lived such sinful, self-gratifying lives that are contrary to God's will and design for us. However, accepting that we are sinners is not easy, since the world doesn't support this type of thinking, especially the new age. But Jesus doesn't love bomb: He shows you the truth.

The guilt of being a spiritual teacher and leading people away from God was something I found especially painful and I was very sorry for my mistake. All this while there was a God who longed to be in relationship with me and His people, and there was I, working with clients and effectively pulling them further away from Him. Praise God for His grace and forgiveness, which has been the biggest blessing in my life! It's a hard thing to accept our error especially when we think we are 'lightworkers'. But just know God is merciful and His grace makes everything beautiful.

While I felt convicted of most of my unholy life, some things had become so normal to me, I just couldn't perceive them as sin or see them in any negative way at all. For instance, "Do not murder" is easy to accept as we know the consequences, so the majority of us are not tempted to commit murder. But there were other sins I didn't see as that bad on the grounds they didn't really hurt anyone. I was really struggling with certain acts and practices I used to be involved in that made me hold back on coming fully into repentance because I didn't understand the depth of them. Yes, I did repent but I wasn't quite sincere about it. It was more of an act driven from the motive I needed to get on the right side of God; but it wasn't full-hearted. So I started to pray on it, "Father, please show me why this sin is so bad. Please show me why You don't want people to sin in this way". And God answers prayer.

The first month of being in my new place, I barely had any furniture – just one sofa surrounded by blank white walls, and a bare floor. It was just me and God, stripped back and personal. This was the night I felt I genuinely came to God as there had been so much blocking our relationship – all this sin that I had previously lived in. I felt God working in me to show me how defiling sin really is. I know some may find this uncomfortable, but that night God showed me the depths of my sin. I felt filthy. I was just remembering all these times I had been working with these spirits and encouraging people to sin. I remember the times I had abused my God-given body, the times I had chosen my own selfish desires over God, running after worldly recognition and prideful pursuits. There was so much worship and praise for myself, worship of other gods and idols, a life of ignorance towards Him – all these things I could now confirm. The small things that were harmless in my mind were making me unholy, damaging my mind and how I viewed others. But, most of all, they were getting in the way of a relationship with God. That day I was gifted to see sin through the eyes of how God sees it, and He was gracious enough to share His sadness with me. I could see how the things I had thought were so spiritual were in reality so dark and conceited.

I dropped to my knees and sobbed, tears pouring from my eyes, the type of cry that makes your stomach ache. I could now see the error of my ways. I was grovelling on the floor, not because I had to but because I wanted to. With a snotty nose, face contorted with weeping, nothing could hold me back now. I was so sorry that I had been rebelling against my God my entire life. And God softened my heart and allowed me to see past my pride, which brought me to my knees. I feel so blessed He worked in me that way and so thankful the entire experience was so comforting. I can't explain what I felt inside my heart the days after this happened. This for me was the experience of being born again. Though I had been through many 're-births' in the New Age, this was not the same. I felt like I had just been born into this world, just come alive. As the Bible says, "Therefore, if anyone *is* in Christ, *he is* a new creation; old things have passed away; behold, all things have become new" (2 Corinthians 5:17). And I knew I was a new creation in my Saviour Jesus Christ.

This was a significant moment in my Christian walk. I had the assurance I had received the gift of new life. I knew Jesus was the only way and I knew that from here on out I just wanted to spend the rest of my life serving Him, following Him, and leading people to Him. In my heart I had experienced the power of His love, acceptance, and forgiveness through His grace on a magnitude that's challenging to describe with any justice. As the prophet Ezekiel said, "I will give you a new heart and put a new spirit within you; I will remove your heart of stone and give you a heart of flesh ... " (Ezekiel 36:26). This is exactly what it felt like. Just as the Bible says we get new hearts, I got mine.

People have said to me, "How can you say most things you did previously were not of God?" I answer that it is because it leads people away from the true God and it hurts to think I was leading people astray. But let's just say it reminds me of the Bible verse where Jesus is talking about the Pharisees, a group of religious leaders who would not receive Him. Jesus says, "they are blind guides. If the blind lead the blind, both will fall into a pit" (Matthew 15:14). I had no idea what I was involved in, and it was heartbreaking to know the real truth. I was so blinded by the positive results I was experiencing that I couldn't see all the lies. The people I led and taught came to me for help and most of them would say they got it. Some still can't understand my choice to follow Christ, and in a way I understand because I thought the same.

I tried to comfort myself as it wasn't as if I knew what I was doing and as soon as I saw the truth I stopped immediately. The bottom line is we were all being deceived: just as I was teaching others, I was also paying others to teach me. I never stopped investing in mentors and programs myself and, believe me, the amount of money I earned was not anywhere near the amount of money I paid others. I never charged in the thousands for my work, but I did pay that. But nothing breaks through like the unvarnished truth: I was a sinner, who had done many sinful things that dishonoured my God. I had to stop making excuses, and get on my knees and repent.

It took me a long time to realise I was forgiven. But that's because, when we realise how much we have turned from our God, we can't understand at first the magnitude of His grace. It's that incredible. This is not about religion. Yes, Christianity by definition is a religion. But Jesus did not like religion, especially when it was legalistic with no heart. No, Christianity is all about a relationship, and like you would need to if you wronged any relationship, you make things right.

My life was so entrenched in sin in the new age, and I'm so thankful Jesus came and rescued me from that life. The sin may have given my flesh some short-term pleasure, but it damaged my spirit. I am eternally grateful He did that for me. He just came into all the destruction around my life and held out His hand. I did nothing to deserve it, and He had every reason not to come get me. But He did. I was in controlling relationships, deceived by spirits, performing witchcraft, full of pride, selfish and self-centred, in sexual sin, encouraging others to sin, and leading them to other gods ... and more. I didn't want to know Jesus all my adult life. I'd spent a lifetime ignoring Him and He still came and got me. How incredible! How pure is His love for us!

The word 'repentance' (Greek: *metanouia*) means 'changing one's mind'. Changing one's mind in this context involves turning away from one's sin and asking for cleansing. And God does just that. He cleanses our minds and hearts so we can see sin for what it is. If you believe, I encourage you to look at your sin, acknowledge it, accept it, and turn away from it like the Bible tells us. But, most of all, repent of it, for the sake of your relationship with God. He is so loving, He will comfort you and be there for you. But you have sinned against Him, and you need to make it right. If you don't feel that sin is a genuine violation of His commandments, pray for Him to show you the depths of your sin. I've come to realise God loves a seeking heart that genuinely wants to know Him and His truths. He wants you to repent, He calls us to repent, but also remember He doesn't want you to stay in that place. Jesus said, "Blessed are those who mourn, for they shall be comforted" (Matthew 5:4).

If you feel moved by this sharing, you can pray this prayer in your heart:

"Dear Father, I pray You open my heart and mind to the sin that is in my life so I can recognise Christ and what is not of You. Help me to turn from my sin and change my ways. Please give me the strength to have victory over the sin. I ask, dear Father, that You work on my heart and sanctify me, so I can become more like Your Son, Jesus. Amen."

"And I will ask the Father, and he will give you another advocate to help you and be with you forever—the Spirit of truth. The world cannot accept him, because it neither sees him nor knows him. But you know him, for he lives with you and will be in you."

John 14:16-17

But What about Reiki?

At this stage I had stopped practising everything that pertained to new age. However, there were some things that I wondered were of God or not. I started to wonder whether I had acted too hastily – *Maybe it didn't **all** need to go?* I told myself. *Because the New Age is truth mixed with lies, perhaps some of the practices were from God and some were not* – well that was my reasoning at the time. But once I researched, prayed, and reflected upon everything I did, I never went back to any of my former practices. Once I searched the scriptures, it was quite easy for to me recognise that Jesus has no connection to reiki.

Reiki used to be a big part of my life. I had championed reiki as one of tools that helped me give up alcohol, so I had an emotional bond with it. It wasn't until I looked back on my reiki journey that I realised the time I really opened up to the spirit realm was after my 'Reiki Two Attunement'. It was then that I saw angel wings in my third eye (the chakra between the eyebrows in eastern practices). I've come to notice that, every time I had a breakthrough in the new age, it was as if that breakthrough was just another big leap further into deception and further away from the truth.

After Reiki Level Two, I felt that I was so connected to the spirit world I could see so much more in my mind's eye. I would often see people as they were in a past life, or, if I was working in a session, spirit would highlight certain parts of the body for me to attend to through my energy. In nature, I would see dragons and I began working with them. Isis I saw often when I worked with her and other goddess energy too. However, once I came to Christ, it all stopped and my reiki attunement disappeared.

I even researched and found out that even the story of Miako Usui, the Founder of Reiki (he claims he 'rediscovered' it), has been widely fabricated. Apparently, he obtained a doctorate degree at the University of Chicago, but research has proven this to be false. As part of my reiki training, I had been taught the history of the energy. I was told Mikao Usui was a Christian teacher and was teaching a Christian class when he was asked by a student, "If we are all made in the image of God and Jesus can heal, then when can we heal like Jesus?" As the story goes, he didn't know the answer to the student's question, so he spent the **his next years** pursuing the answer. He ended up meditating amongst a group of monks; that was when he received an attunement from a higher power. I always used to find this odd even as a new ager. While I didn't have an in-depth knowledge of Christianity, I knew enough to know that, when they look for answers, they turn to the God in the Bible and not to a Buddhist monastery.

Hawayo Takata, one of the earliest reiki masters, was responsible for bringing reiki to the West. There are reports that her claim of Maiko being Christian and linking the story to Jesus was fabricated so as to make reiki palatable to a Western audience. Takata was a resident of Hawaii, which has a large Christian community and therefore linking reiki to Jesus was to make it more readily accepted – and it was. However, later evidence showed that reiki had come from a solid Buddhist background with Gautama Buddha believed to be the source.

Like most new agers, I had heard that Jesus had travelled to India and Tibet to learn reiki. In the Bible there is a gap between Jesus' growing up years (from age twelve to thirty) and His ministry; these eighteen years are known as the unknown years. So the theory goes, during this time Jesus travelled to the Far East to study reiki with Buddhist and Hindu followers. It's actually a heresy perpetuated in new age circles, something that's pure speculation with no evidence to back it up. We would just say it, because that's what we heard and it seemed plausible.

However, we can trace one rumour back to a book written by Nicolas Novotich in 1858. Nicolas claims that Jesus spent six years in East Asia, studying the sacred texts. Now this I find a very far leap considering Jesus consistently quoted the Old Testament and no other 'sacred' document. Nicolas later admitted he had fabricated the entire story but, apparently this false information still circulates. There's something enticing about information coming to us that we think is hidden knowledge unknown to the masses, and the different variations of 'Jesus' in the new age takes advantage of this.

We don't fully know what happened in the unknown years of Jesus because the Bible does not mention them. However, I've come to know that if the full details are not in the Bible it's because God doesn't consider it necessary for us to know. Scripture does, however, give a convincing indication He grew up in His home town of Nazareth. In the gospel of Luke, after the birth of Jesus the Bible states "... and when they had performed everything according to the Law of the Lord, they returned to Galilee, to their own town of Nazareth. And the child grew and became strong, filled with wisdom. And the favor of God was upon Him." Not only that, but throughout the gospel of Matthew and Luke, it is evident He was brought up in the Jewish faith observing all its laws and customs and submitting to the teachings. The theory He went to any location in the Far East is a serious stretch, with no evidence that remotely suggests this ever happened.

It's clear to me from scripture and from how I've seen God work in people that He shapes one's character mainly through circumstances. We see this in Luke 4 when the Holy Spirit led Jesus into the wilderness to be tempted by the devil. See Jesus was God, but also man, and so He did have temptations of the flesh as the verse specifically says Jesus was "tempted". This shows, even though He was sinless, He did have to battle with His human nature, which would lead me to believe that God had been shaping His character for many years. The Father does this throughout scripture. For instance, Moses was called whilst tending to sheep. Joshua, Samuel, they all went through training for their purpose within the Kingdom and God launched their ministry only when they were ready. In fact, Hebrews 2:10 says, "Everything belongs to God, and all things were created by his power. So God did the right thing when he made Jesus perfect by suffering, as Jesus led many of God's children to be saved and to share in his glory". So God made Jesus **perfect** through suffering. We know that Jesus as Son of God was already perfect, but the element of suffering as a man gave Him first-hand exposure to the human condition.

As for Jesus' healing, when I searched the scriptures, I found Jesus confirmed that His healing was through the Holy Spirit. In Matthew 12, the Pharisees accused Him of working with the devil, and Jesus' response was "You just blasphemed the Holy Spirit". As a new Christian I knew that the only spirit that is of God is the Holy Spirit, and I was not interested in any other spirit.

So how do we receive the Holy Spirit? We received Him the moment we confessed Jesus as Lord and Saviour because the Bible says we are then sealed with the Holy Spirit: "In him you also, when you heard the word of truth, the gospel of your salvation, and believed in him, were sealed with the promised Holy Spirit" (Ephesians 1:13). What is a seal? A seal is a mark that validates the ownership of something. The promised Holy Spirit is that seal that validates God's people as His inheritance. The experience of the Holy Spirit in a believer's life provides the inward assurance that they belong to God as His children; it also demonstrates to others the genuineness of their faith.

But why is it there is no way that Jesus could be practising reiki? Easy. Because reiki is not of the Holy Spirit: it's counterfeit power. If we can only receive the Holy Spirit by knowing Jesus, and there are millions of people attuned to reiki without knowing Jesus, then what is the spirit they 'attune' to?

Jesus said the Holy Spirit was a helper, and that the Holy Spirit was to direct people to Him. In John 15, Jesus describes the Holy Spirit as the Helper: "he is the Spirit of truth who comes from the Father. When he comes, he will tell about me, and you also must tell people about me, because you have been with me from the beginning." Jesus said the Holy Spirit will point people to Him. It is evident that reiki energy does not point people to Jesus Christ. There are many reiki practitioners who do not know Jesus or want to. There are also Christians practising reiki believing it's the Holy Spirit. But, based on the facts, how can their power come from the Holy Spirit? The energy doesn't change by the receiver adopting another faith regardless of the intention: it's either the Holy Spirit or it isn't. There are only two sources of spiritual power in this world: so, if it's not God, then it's Satan.

On the other hand, the Bible often speaks of the laying on of hands for healing or empowering as a spiritual gift of the Holy Spirit (see

1 Corinthians 12 for gifts of the Holy Spirit). This is a gift that **believers** may receive after receiving Christ as Lord and Saviour. The fact that most people pay for a reiki attunement (I know I did) makes it clear it's not a spiritual **gift.** Jesus never performed an attunement on His disciples, never 'set up' an energy session, never drew pagan symbols over someone in order to heal them. No, His disciples received the gift through the power of the Holy Spirit, **because they believed.**

How did Jesus give them the Holy Spirit? He breathed on them; "And with that he breathed on them and said, 'Receive the Holy Spirit'" (John 20:22). I found this amazing, as Jesus brings life; He claimed to be the way, the truth and the life. When we go back to the beginning of time to Genesis, we see God created man and then He breathed His spirit into them to give them life "The Lord God formed man of the dust of the ground, and breathed into his nostrils the breath of life; and the man became a living soul" (Genesis 2:7). Then sin entered the world and we were separated from God. Then Jesus was born into flesh to walk the earth and bridge that gap. He breathed life back into the disciples and said to them: "Receive the Holy Spirit" (John 20:22). Only Jesus could breathe life into them because He is God!

Needless to say, Jesus didn't bring, teach or learn reiki. It's a counterfeit source of energy, admittedly a good one, but a counterfeit nonetheless.

"Sanctify them in the truth; your word is truth."

John 17:17

Reflections through Christ

I do reflect on my time in the New Age and can feel gratitude for many things that happened in that time. I stopped drinking and partying; I met some lovely people and went through some important life lessons. Because the movement is a concoction of truth mixed with lies, positive things do occur. I would hate to think where my life would have been if I continued to take cocaine, drink alcohol, and smoke cigarettes. There is an aspect where I did partake in these pleasures for the sake of spiritual experiences – after all, recreational drugs and alcohol are a form of escapism. Some of us go through times where our problems, issues, trauma, and health are so overwhelming we just find a quick means to escape from it all, and the New Age offers this means to escape our reality, especially in journeying or energy sessions. But, in general, it encourages us to reject reality as I now know it.

Because of Christ, I can now reflect on my relationship with Toni in such a different way. I have chosen not to give the exact details of the relationship, one, to protect the person's identity and, secondly, it would reveal some very personal things, most of which involve sin and do not glorify God. Since the Holy Spirit has walked me in the path of truth, I no longer look back on that relationship and feel like the victim. I just look back and see two sinners, so far away from God, so deep in sin that they couldn't even find a way out. Thankfully, there was a way out in Jesus Christ. That relationship made me aware of how much we can be deceived, how we can feel such high and electrifying emotions; but they are not the truth. I learnt that Satan works in people to lead us further away from God, and there's no denying, Satan had a hold of me too.

On the other hand, when we have the Holy Spirit dwelling within us, it sanctifies us and reveals the truth of our hearts. The truth is I also showed narcissistic traits in the relationship. When Toni was slipping away, I resorted to manipulation, attempting to control and play games. Sure, it wasn't to the same degree and the motivation was different – more out of fear and desperation to restore the relationship. However, the bottom line is I wasn't a healthy person to be in a relationship with: my belief system was confused and certainly contributed to the toxic stew it had become. I've come to learn that I was no better than Toni. Would I have said I was a good person back then? Yes. But the reality is I was also a sinner who needed Christ. The only thing that sets me apart from Toni now is that I now walk in the righteousness of Christ. And that's not on my own merit: it's all Jesus.

As a result of my beliefs, I had become self-centred and had an inflated ego. I really believed what my guides used to tell me: that I was someone special who was here specifically for the ascension. I heard it so much in energy sessions that I was convinced it was true. I was told that I had been important figures in history in past lives. Deep down, I thought I was just humble for not declaring my famous histories publicly. But then, introduce a man to the mix and, all of a sudden, I had to work to keep his love, which obviously showed my confidence was only superficial.

When I look back on that relationship, the entire reason why I fell so hard was because of the way Toni made me feel ... about myself. He inflated me that bit more, made me feel more special and more powerful, and I liked it. Argh, it's the ugly truth, but there it is! Moreover, the teachings I was following were just reinforcing my self-centredness. I was even deluded enough to believe that the courses of some of my family members' lives had gone awry because of the lessons I could learn from them. Imagine, other people's experiences evolving around me! But this wasn't put in an obvious way. It's sneaky the way the teachings make you feel so elevated, like you witness what you see before you, then own it by clearing your own blocks to heal. But what about them?

Even today, I've reflected so much about the way we're taught about relationships: it's all about ourselves. It's all about getting your needs met. If you're not getting what you want, you have the right to leave. We do not ask ourselves some very pertinent questions. Are we as calculating with ourselves as with the other person? What are we doing to meet the other person's needs? What is it like to be in a relationship with us? How do our actions impact them? For now, I have yet to enter a romantic relationship whilst in Christ. When I do, it will be with the intent to marry. God has revealed to me how a godly character in a man is essential just as it's essential for me to be a woman of God, something He is still shaping me into.

The new age makes everything about us so spiritual!! The best way we can help humanity is by becoming the best version of ourselves, by reaching enlightenment. We are continuously clearing our chakras, releasing trauma, calling back gifts from past lives, releasing blocks. We are willing participants in sound healing, crystal healing, journeying, plant medicine, activations, downloads, light language, spirit guides, light family, sage burning, constant triggers and releasing emotions, sacred dance – the list goes on – all as a way for our true selves to emerge. It's all about us. In my new walk with Christ, I've come to realise it's not about me: it's about God.

I've also learnt to put my emotions in their proper perspective and found the meaning of true love. I don't love Christ based on how I'm feeling; I don't love Christ based on whether I get what I want either. I did not deserve salvation. I spent my entire life indulging in things that God hates. I was so deep in sin I couldn't see any other way of living and, even though I never wanted to know Him, even though I had rejected Him, did things that mocked Him, and I didn't ask for it, He still came for me. That's love.

As you can see, I've had to face some hard truths in my walk with the Lord. Half of my lack of responsibility was based on excuses: I simply thought I was way too cosmic and free spirited for any type of discipline in my life. One area in which I was irresponsible was my finances. I allowed myself to get more and more into debt without facing the hard truths about my financial situation. I spent all my own money on courses, programs, sessions, retreats, materials in search of the next level. Whenever my money ran out, I used my credit cards to the max, and was certainly living beyond my means. I remember once paying £350 for a crystal necklace on a credit card. I don't know how in my head I justified that but I thought this was one special crystal that was going to give me some sort of shift, so it was worth the investment. I remember telling myself I just needed that next course, and then I would stop spending. Then I would be at the next level vibration, and sold into the next course with the same coach and out came the credit card again. I wasn't stewarding my money well and the Lord has shown me this. All this spending was driven by the triggers and the constant highs and lows, the energetic upgrades, and the ascension symptoms. The difference in my energy since being saved has been like comparing night and day. Now that my moods and emotions are so stable, it confirms to me that I definitely wasn't the one in charge of my 'energy'.

When I was studying the dynamics of narcissism, I came to discover that, if we are susceptible to narcissism, we are usually co-dependent. Co-dependency is essentially placing our worth and value on how we are being treated and responded to in our relationships. How we feel about ourselves can easily change based on the treatment we receive from others. It can lead to looking to others for approval, which then affects how we live and feel about ourselves. It's depending on others in areas like finance, career, decision making – even the smaller things like whom we listen to or what we watch. Deeper still, co-dependency is also being unable to separate ourselves from the other party's emotions and feelings. So we may be having a good day but we become depressed just because they are. We feel guilty if we're happy and they're not. Of course, we are not aware of the dynamics at the time. I know that I always spoke up and shared my spiritual journey with the motive of helping others, but also, I was looking to be liked and admired – I wasn't aware of this, but it's true.

As I researched co-dependency, I came across quite a few professionals online and they all claimed to have 'the cure' or the healing remedy. Every single one was pointing me to more inner child work, something I'd been doing non-stop for four years. Inner child work is something that I've come to see as just another step in the wrong direction. We are trying to mend that little child inside of us, trying to deal with the trauma of feeling unloved, unheard, and unseen during childhood, but essentially, we are getting back on the hamster wheel. We are trying to re-parent ourselves, so to speak, but I truly believe it's the love of our heavenly Father we are truly yearning for. All these emotions I had been clearing in the New Age were not of God but a result of the fall of our first parents. They were compounded by sin and wrong choices.

The solution to most problems in the New Age is to clear all guilt and shame. But it still doesn't tackle the root problem of how they got there. The core issue is being separated from God. That's why the New Age is never ending. The healing helps; it brings some results, but it will never reach the main issue, that connection and relationship with the One True Living God. That's the missing link that's only found in God.

In my opinion, true healing cannot happen without Jesus Christ. As we receive Jesus' atonement through the work of the Cross, we come back home. He is our Provider, our Protector, our Healer, our Shepherd, our Maker. We are trying so desperately to tap into the human psyche to try and figure out how we can heal and move forward, but it's clearly a broken connection.

And it's so wonderful when that connection is restored. We don't have to meditate for hours to feel peace. We don't have to clear all our childhood wounds to experience joy. We don't have to manifest our dream home and car to know we're truly rich. We just need Jesus. Jesus didn't just come to give us new life so we can constantly try to patch up the old one. No, He offered us a total transformation through the renewing of our mind. When I received God's grace to make Jesus the Lord of my life, all the clearing, releasing, and constant self-examination seemed so extreme and unhealthy to me. I now see the way I lived as so bizarre.

I'm not suggesting for a second that reflection on deep traumas in childhood is not necessary. If you need to process certain aspects of your life or talk to a professional about this, I encourage you to discuss this openly with someone. There is power in sharing in a safe non-judgemental setting. But I'm amazed at the miracles Jesus brings just by living in Him. No power can match this.

I've found that walking in the presence of the Bread of life, the True Vine, The Light of the World, our Redeemer, Jesus Christ, we can be changed supernaturally **just by being in His presence** – no appointment necessary. You start anew with Christ, baptised with the Holy Spirit. All that old baggage is buried in the grave as our old self dies, and our new spirit is resurrected in Him! That's all I've ever needed: His Word, His Promises, His Love, His Grace, His Forgiveness, His Truth, His Strength. I've found it!

God also heals through circumstances too. He puts you in situations where you have no choice but to break through. He even starts preparing us for change! I see this with my dog, Gaia. She has been such an important part of my transition from heavy new age to now. Pointers are my favourite dog but I always said I'd probably never have one as they are too big. One day, without invitation, a medium-sized cross breed little dog with a pointer coat appeared on my doorstep looking for a home. I just knew she was mine. This dog has been such a blessing, not just because she was my comfort through the storms, but because if it weren't for her I would never have faced my lack of financial responsibility and dependency on others. It would have been so much more stress-free to go into a house share again and split the costs. I'd left home when I was twenty-one and rented with others all the way up to thirty-six. But with my dog, I knew I needed my own place. Having her, forced me to become dependent on God and to learn how to live within my means. God had already prepared to heal my co-dependency before I even knew about it through that little dog.

My friend, God will give you His strength too. Things I once feared, like being rejected or mocked, I was able to confront because His love overcomes all fear. God's words in the Bible begin to change you as they permeate your soul, verse by verse. Jesus said, "I am the vine; you are the branches. If you remain in me and I in you, you will bear much fruit; apart from me you can do nothing" (John 15:1). We just need to remain in Christ and walk with Him – that's all we need. The person I am now compared to the person I was is nothing short of a miracle; it's a change that no amount of healing session could have done.

When I look at my old life I can see things so much more clearly now. I remember how I once had to remind myself daily to sit down and write a gratitude list. I had to plan to be grateful. Now it's just part of my walk. My tears will often well up at the love of Christ, the beauty of God's creation and the overwhelming comfort of His presence, and this brings spontaneous words of gratitude for what my Saviour has done for me.

What I did not expect when coming to Christ was the degree of peace and joy I would feel in my heart from day by day. Most people from the New Age who have now made Jesus their Lord claim the same peace and joy, something that took them by complete surprise. It's easy to feel happy when outside circumstances are going great, but it also comes as a complete shock when you're facing uncertainty, or even chaos, and you just feel peace and joy. But that's Jesus, the Vine.

"So that your faith might not rest on human wisdom, but on God's power."

1 Corinthians 2:5

Jeremiah 29:11

Leaving my new age life behind was daunting and unlike anything I'd ever experienced. This time it wasn't a case of going through another 'shift' or 'stepping into the unknown'. I was becoming 'a child of God'. But that didn't mean the transition was comfortable, even though God was there every step of the way.

You see, I was so grateful for my salvation, but at the same time I felt I had lost a big part of my identity. I understand now how that's not true, but it seemed like that at the time. How God had made me never changed, but I had chosen to add layers of disguise upon myself because I trying too hard to find 'myself'. I had built a lifestyle around my New Age beliefs, and my daily routine was evolved around it. Now the morning rituals, the friends I met up with regularly to do energy work with, the books I read, my kind of business, all that had to leave my life. All the crystals, oracle cards, sage, yoga mat, books and, sadly, even some friends who had trouble accepting my new faith had to go. Who was I now? What was my purpose?

The good news is that my life in Christ had not stopped: it had just begun! Jesus meant it when He said He comes to give us life and life more abundantly (John 10:10). God has a purpose and plan for all of us. He tells us we are "wonderfully and fearfully made" ... for He "knitted us in our mother's womb" (Psalm 139:13,14). In fact, when you look at your skin under a microscope, you can actually see that our skin is woven, just like this verse says. You are made by Him, like no one else; your fingerprints do not a match anyone else's. So yes you have purpose; He created you with one.

There are two aspects that I've personally found to this purpose. The first one is what I call the Primary Purpose. Scripture shows us that God created man primarily for relationship with Him and ultimately to bring Him glory. That's it. By communing with Him daily, in prayer, worship, reading His Word, and staying faithful to the word, you are living out such a purpose. And, like any relationship, as that develops, the Father is going to reveal more of Himself, His Son and the Holy Spirit to you. I can testify that it's going to be so overwhelmingly special. Like any relationship, you have to commit to where He is leading you. He will use you and work with you to reach others and bring glory to Him. This is your calling or Secondary Purpose. But we can't skip to the secondary without first establishing relationship.

How God will choose to work in you will be unique to you. But one thing I know for sure: if you truly desire the Lord to use you to reach others (saved people have a heart for the lost), then you must realise that it's all Him. You just need to be willing to completely submit to His will in how He desires to use you. He will shape your character and, if there's some correction that's needed, He will help you face this head on, and guide you through this process by the Holy Spirit. Remember, sanctification means to become holy and set apart for His purpose. When we are saved, God begins to work on building us to equip us for the assignment(s) He has planned for our lives.

Looking back, I see how my guides always used to badger me into stepping up my lightworker role. The message was always along the lines of promoting me with more power, more enlightenment, more recognition. "It's time for you to step into your power. It's time for you to own who you are. Remember who you are. You've been training lifetimes for this – it's your time and you're here to help humanity," they would urge.

How different this is from a genuine call from God! When we are called by God, it's only about two things, Him and/or His people. When God calls you, He shares with you His sadness for what He sees in people – He shares His heart with you. More often than not, He asks you to do something at first you don't think you're capable of doing. In fact, much of the time, you don't want to do it as you think God has chosen wrong. That's a good place to be, as then you'll realise you can't do it alone. But God can, and you know you'll have to just let Him work in you through and through. Faith is staying faithful to God and His word. Trust me when I say, "Don't get distracted." I can't stress enough how important this is.

Unfortunately, there are false teachers operating under the banner of Christianity who are out there to deceive the sheep. This is something else Jesus warns us about in the Sermon on the Mount, "Beware of false prophets. They come in sheep's clothing, but inwardly they are ravenous wolves" (Matthew 7:15). I can tell you as a Christian, nothing will try and take you off your path like false teaching and nothing is more likely to succeed as this. Once we are saved, the next interest of the enemy is to make us ineffective in the Body of Christ, especially in reaching out to the lost. Don't get caught up in distractions from messengers of Satan.

God has reminded me of my uniqueness without leading me down a path of superiority. He has reminded me of how He made me and what makes me special. When we receive the Holy Spirit, we receive the gifts of the Spirit: some may receive spiritual discernment, some the gift of prophecy or teaching, some the gift of healing (see 1 Corinthians 12). These gifts are meant to edify others. But here I'm referring to God-given talents I identified in myself at a young age. With inner child work, I used to connect back to my childhood hobbies – but this wasn't the same. God reminded me of the gifts I was born with, it had to do with how I was made. One day I remembered a newspaper clipping I had when I raced well as a kid. I won the Essex championships, and the head line was 'Super Sarah-Jayne'. You can imagine how it felt at the age of eleven to have your name mentioned in the paper for something you loved to do. I really wanted to read the newspaper article again. I tried to search the gazette archives but with no luck, but I really wanted to reconnect with that experience. I prayed to God and asked if He could unite me with a copy of the write-up. Three months passed and, to be honest, I had completely forgotten about the newspaper clipping and the prayer.

Then one afternoon my mum came to visit. In her hand was a bag. She had found some old scrap books in a box under her bed. And guess what was is in it ... yes, you guessed!. Not a copy, but the original paper clipping! That eleven-year-old little girl had cut it out herself and glued it into her scrap book! Not only that but accompanying it, in the same bag, was every single one of my school reports from junior school to senior. I read through them all. There were so many rich memories and I was starting to remember certain things for the first time. Running was not my only gift; there was my art and also many things in my character I had never seen before and are still so present in me today. Each one of us is born with unique gifts, talents and leanings. They are given to believers and non-believers alike.

I didn't realise until writing this book how much regret I had felt for not utilising my gifts at an early age. I had God-given gifts; I was talented in certain areas just like everyone else. I've come to realise I can use these gifts for His purpose, for the Kingdom. How much better than following my own passions and pleasures! His Kingdom is now my passion: bringing glory to Him and pointing people to Christ. The last time I saw this scrapbook must have been well over twenty years ago! Now I was looking at it and saw all the promise. There was so much in there I had forgotten about myself, and I praise the Father for reminding me who I really am before alcohol, before drugs and before the New Age tried to steal that from me. He made us all with intention, purpose, and love. How did He make you?

> "'For I know the plans I have for you,' declares the Lord, 'plans to prosper you and not to harm you, plans to give you hope and a future'" (Jeremiah 29:11).

Will you join me in this prayer?

"Dear Heavenly Father, You created me in my mother's womb. You are my Maker and I know my primary purpose is to be in relationship with You. Please bring me closer to You, Lord. I pray our relationship deepens and I pray when the time is right, You will call me for Your purpose to reach others and bring glory to You and Your Kingdom. In Jesus' name I pray."

"Do not fear, for I am with you; Do not anxiously look about you, for I am your God. I will strengthen you, surely I will help you, Surely I will uphold you with My righteous right hand."

Isaiah 41:10

A Heads Up

Thank you for being open to reading this book. I quite understand that some of you may disagree with what I have shared, but I truly believe many more will read my story and it will connect to so much of what is happening in their life. I've been praying for months for God to start preparing those for whom it is His will to read this book. I believe, if that is His will, then God would have started a work in you some time ago. If you are one of those people, then this chapter is for you.

To be clear, I have been a Christian now for two years. I'm by no means mature in my faith but what I share in this chapter is what I've come to know in my own walk that may be helpful for those new in the faith too. Know that God will always provide for you. There are so many things He has worked out in my favour when the odds were stacked against me. It can be very scary leaving a business that you've put a lot of time and effort into. So, whatever your situation, if you follow Christ, He will support you; it may not be in the way you predict, but He will never forsake you.

When I moved into my cottage, that's when I truly realised everything I had done was through deception. I stopped all those practices overnight. I decided to clear all the spiritual stuff out of my business and just work on helping new start-up coaches and mentors build programs online. It was a bit up and down; sometimes the money would come, sometimes it wouldn't. I was going through so many challenges, and I knew I didn't have the time and energy to build a new client base whilst worrying if I could pay my rent. On top of that, the clients I was attracting were New Agers too, and this didn't make me feel good. Just because I was not directly practising New Age, I don't think helping people promote their new age business is what God had in mind for the clients or myself.

So, I prayed. I prayed for consistent income to support me living in the cottage, to not have to worry about bills and be stressed every week when my rent was due. But there was one problem: I couldn't see me being able to get a full-time job as I couldn't leave my dog alone for eight hours a day. The local day care centre had limited resources for minding her. My situation felt hopeless, but I trusted God would be faithful. I just prayed; that's all I could do as I didn't know what direction to take. But I did know I couldn't part from Gaia; she had been my faithful companion the entire way through this. I would rather be broke than have to give her up.

To my surprise, I got a call from my brother. He knew a company hiring with jobs working from home. I put my CV forward and started the position the following week. I never would have even thought of a home-based job. I wasn't even aware they did that for my skillset; but God provided for me, and the money was the exact amount I needed to pay all my bills and with just a little left over every month. Praise the Lord!! He always provides.

If fear overwhelms you, get closer to God. As a Christian, the Bible needs to be our source of strength. Reading His word is key. Pray before we open it for God to enter a conversation with us, to fill us with the Holy Spirit so we can understand what He is saying to us in the moment, and we can hear Him clearly. There have been occasions where a verse will just hit me with a wave of truth, a realisation or breakthrough, just as if God is speaking directly to me. We have the Holy Spirit to thank for that.

Joshua chapter 1 carried me through my first three months of salvation, "I will be with you, I will never leave you nor forsake you ... Be strong and courageous. Do not be afraid; do not be discouraged, for the Lord your God will be with you wherever you go" (Joshua 1:5, 9). If you're someone who has left New Age for Christ, the beginning of the journey can feel chaotic. Satan doesn't want to let you go that easily. Let God's direct words to you carry you through. Remind yourself that He is with you; He's always there and ready to fight your battles for you. Remember you don't have to *feel* He is there to know **He is there**. Gone are the days when feelings determined the reality of the situation. If you put your faith in Christ, the fact is you have chosen to follow the One True Living God and He is in control, He is faithful. You can put your faith in Him and His word and stand on that.

Do you know, the command "Do not fear" is in the Bible 365 times? That's one "Do not fear" for every day. This is a command, not a comfort, because there really is no reason to fear. When you've committed yourself and the works of your hands to God, He will provide; He will take care of you as His beloved child. Much easier said than done I know. But He assures as in His word "Commit your actions to the LORD, and your plans will succeed" (Proverbs 16:3). Of course, there will be times of fear, sadness, anger, grief, frustration and loss of confidence. But use those times to go to Him with it all ... it will deepen your relationship and it will strengthen your faith when you see He truly answers prayers and is listening. "God will meet all your needs according to the riches and glory in Jesus Christ" (Philippians 4:19).

You can count on Him. I've seen so many people come out of New Age and it never ceases to amaze me how He continues to work in people's lives. It's truly a blessing just to witness. My walk with God has not been perfect, but every time things have gone downhill, it's usually because I lost faith in God and I took matters into my own hands. There were times when I felt like He had forgotten about me or just hadn't heard my prayers. Please believe me when I say, now I know, this was when He was working the most. I just couldn't feel or see it and well ... that's not faith. As the Apostle Paul wrote, "We walk by faith and not by sight" (2 Corinthians 5:7). This is one truth I've come to know and love.

We are all loved, every single one of us. So loved He died for us: you are that important to Him. He has shown me what love truly is and He is demonstrates that genuine love. I never knew true love until I came to know Jesus. The magnitude of His sacrificial love is sometimes hard for me to fully comprehend. But it's important to mention. The message of the gospel does not bend to the will of the world – not our own will either. The New Age is still another way of saying, "Come this way; this is how you get what you want". But I've seen people come to Christ because they realise the deception there. They realise it is spiritually fruitless and demonic, but they turn to Christ as by a means of *getting what they want*. This is not the true message in the Bible.

God blesses us in ways we never dreamed of, but when we come to Christ we lay down our own desires and follow His will for our lives. There will be blessings but that doesn't always feed our own desires, and there will be times when we battle with what we want and what God is calling us to do. This is your walk of obedience. The way He blesses us is something true and pure; but it may not be in the way you initially desired or expected. That's where faith in Him is everything. Psalm 37:4 states, "Take delight in the Lord, and he will give you *the desires of your heart*." Trust that He knows your heart and its desires more than you do. Of course, it can be scary when we are walking in a direction we didn't plan out ourselves; but it's trusting His plan is better than ours and is for His higher purpose. Therefore, walk the course your Creator had planned for you!

Above all, remember that following Jesus is a relationship, not a religion. Christianity is a religion by worldly definition; however, in its essence it is about the relationship we have with God. Jesus came so you can be reconciled with the Father and develop a relationship with Him, not so you could just go to church and sing hymns. See, religion is just action with no heart, a set of rules and rituals we go through to produce a sense of self-righteousness. But being a true believer is experiencing a change of heart, a yearning and an ache to know the heart of God. It is a desire to reach the lost, a desire to be like Christ with His humility that the world cannot comprehend. True faith is where our heart changes, the Holy Spirit grows within us, and we walk the path of sanctification (or separation from worldly things). Then this changes our actions, our thoughts and our attitude towards ourselves and others.

Jesus did not like religion and rebuked the religious nature demonstrated in the Pharisees. Our works are evidence of our faith in Christ – I mean, if you truly follow Christ there would be visible changes in your behaviour. But at the same time, works can't act as a replacement of faith – good works have to be birthed out of our faith.

"For it is by grace you have been saved, through faith—and this is not from yourselves, it is the gift of God—not by works, so that no one can boast. For we are God's handiwork, created in Christ Jesus to do good works, which God prepared in advance for us to do" (Ephesians 2:8-10).

Cultivate a relationship with God. Pray for the things of the spirit, for the heart to be changed and to know who Jesus truly is. Find a Bible-preaching church; it's important you have fellowship on this walk – it's not one to be done alone. I can't tell you how important it is to have faith-filled bible-believing Christians around you. It's good to question everything that is preached and check the scriptures – to keep us from stumbling.

There is so much of my story that I have not shared in this book. The Divine Feminine movement is something I've purposely steered away from as that would warrant another book in itself, but I have so much hope in what I have shared here. I've intentionally left out my visit to France, the belief I was a 'Magdalene' and New Age theories about Mary Magdalene. That's another area of deception to be discussed another time – maybe in another book. But for now, I've come to the end of my testimony for this book. My hope for you is that the Holy Spirit has spoken to you through my story. My hope is that truth is revealed to you in your heart, mind, soul, and spirit. My hope for you is to come to know Jesus Christ for who He truly is, for what He did for you, and how much He truly loves you. You are loved deeply by many I'm sure, but no one is going to love you like Jesus.

We are all on our own journeys, but there is only one path. I pray to God that you find it, choose it, and walk it, to where I hope we meet in eternity.

There's just one last thing I want you to know. When I received my calling from the Lord, I was deep in prayer and asked, "How do You want to use me, Father?"

The voice was clear, "I want My people to know I am their God."

I hope this book helped in some way to do just that.

Final Thoughts

The day of truth is coming; Jesus is returning. It is best to make peace with this truth now before He returns:

> Therefore God also has highly exalted Him and given Him the name which is above every name, that at the name of Jesus every knee should bow, of those in heaven, and of those on earth, and of those under the earth, and *that* every tongue should confess that Jesus Christ *is* Lord, to the glory of God the Father.

Philippians 2:9-11

Paul's prayer for the Ephesians is also my prayer for you:

"And I pray that you, being rooted and established in love, may have power, together with all the Lord's holy people, to grasp how wide and long and high and deep is the love of Christ, and to know this love that surpasses knowledge – that you may be filled to the measure of all the fullness of God."

Ephesians 3:17-19

Printed in Great Britain
by Amazon

28944806R00119